ECOLOGICAL RELATIONSHIPS

ECOLOGICAL RELATIONSHIPS

N. GILBERT
Institute of Animal Resource Ecology,
University of British Columbia

A. P. GUTIERREZ
University of California, Davis

B. D. FRAZER
Canada Agriculture, Vancouver Research Station

R. E. JONES
University of California, Davis

W. H. Freeman and Company
READING AND SAN FRANCISCO

Typeset by Malvern Typesetting Services
Printed in Great Britain by
Fletcher & Son Ltd., Norwich

'To inveftigate, with any tolerable degree of fuccefs, the more retired and diftant parts of the animal oeconomy, is a tafk of no fmall difficulty. An inquiry fo defirable and fo eminently ufeful would require the united efforts of many to give it the defired fuccefs.'

BEWICK (1797)

PREFACE

This book describes one approach to population ecology. We shall analyse the parts of an ecological relationship, and put them together to make a coherent whole. Although it is simple and direct, rather few ecologists have tried this approach.

To put the parts together, we shall often use computer simulation models. Regrettably, many so-called 'simulation models' resemble no ecological relationship known to God or man. By contrast, the strictly realistic models used here will summarize our knowledge of animals and plants observed in the field. They close the gap between fictitious mathematical theories on the one hand and uncoordinated data collection on the other. For historical reasons, our examples all concern insects and their host plants, but the ecological arguments apply in principle to all animals and all plants.

The technical problems of field work and synthesis have now been overcome, but it is still far too early to say how far this approach to ecological research can take us. The reasons for adopting it are considered in the first chapter, and the basic methodology in the second. Chapter 3 links our ecological work to the Darwin–Fisher genetical theory of natural selection. The next four chapters examine the problems presented by various kinds of ecological relationships. Chapter 8 takes a hard look at the merits and limitations of this approach, both for pure research and for management. Part 1 is therefore an overview of the whole approach.

Part 2 shows 'how the trick is done'. Like Part 1, it demands no mathematical expertise of the reader. Chapters 9 and 10 describe, step by step, the construction of a realistic population model. Successive versions of the Fortran program are listed so that the reader may, if he wishes, examine in detail how the successive pieces of biological information are estimated and built into the model: but the argument may be followed

Preface

without any knowledge of Fortran. Chapter 11 examines the technical problems presented by the various kinds of ecological relationship discussed in Part 1.

The methods used in this book derive from – and tie together – the pioneering work of C. S. Holling, R. D. Hughes and R. F. Morris. We are indebted to all three, to our numerous helpers and to our even more numerous critics. We are most grateful to Dr Hughes, to Dr Carl Huffaker, to Mrs Betty Lee and especially to Dr Edward Broadhead for carefully reviewing the manuscript. They do not always agree with what we say! Dr Penelope Ives has not only reviewed the text, but has supplied several important pieces of evidence, used to develop the argument. Chapters 6, 7 and 8 invoke her work. We thank the Editor of the Journal of Animal Ecology for permission to reproduce Fig. 10.3. The National Research Council of Canada, Agriculture Canada Research Branch, the National Science Foundation of the United States of America and the Commonwealth Scientific and Industrial Research Organization, Australia, paid for much of the work discussed here. Whether they got their money's worth must be a matter of opinion.

N.G.
A.P.G.
B.D.F.
R.E.J.

CONTENTS

PART 1

1 INTRODUCTION

If we compare a biochemistry textbook with an ecology textbook, we find that the biochemistry text contains a mass of detailed information, linked together by general principles to form a coherent theory. The ecology book, by contrast, contains a series of disconnected case-histories, often too flimsy to support any certain conclusions, and too varied or too few to yield valid generalizations. Yet both subjects deal with complex biological interactions, and both have been intensively studied since the turn of the century. We do not seek to belittle the efforts of our predecessors. Faced with enormous technical difficulties, they adopted such approaches to the subject as seemed most reasonable at the time; nor can it be said that current approaches to ecological research are, in general, much more successful than were the pioneering attempts. Indeed, the ecological journals today contain even more short-cut panaceas – r- and K-selection, community matrices and so on – than they did thirty years ago, when arguments about density-dependence held the field. We do not suggest that ecologists are more gullible than other scientists; but we cannot help suspecting that many ecologists, and notably those who are averse to working in the field, do not fully appreciate the difficulties that confront us.

Whatever the reason, it remains true that, of the many different approaches to ecological research so far tried, very few have produced any worthwhile results at all, and most have encountered insuperable technical difficulties. This is true both on the academic side of the subject and in its practical applications. Current methods of fishery management, of biological control, and so on, are largely of the 'try-it-and-see' variety. (They are none the worse for that, but perhaps could be much better if we understood more of the underlying ecology.) In this unrewarding situation we need to reconsider

Introduction

what we are trying to do, and how we might best attempt it.

If asked what the subject is about, an ecologist will reply that it is about the relationships between plants, animals and their physical environment – or some such answer. Yet in the past, ecologists have put the animals or plants first and the relationships second. The plants and animals occupy the centre of the stage, while the relationships are a secondary consideration. As long as ecologists insist on placing the organisms first and the relationships second, so long will they be frustrated by technical difficulties. No biochemist would work in this way: there are protein chemists and RNA chemists, but no rat biochemists or *E. coli* chemists as such. In this book, we shall put the ecological relationships first and the organisms second. We shall choose whatever species are convenient to analyse a chosen type of relationship. This change of emphasis, from organism to relationship, is at first sight trivial – but it has far-reaching consequences. It may be objected that, if we want to know how to catch more salmon, we must work on salmon: no use studying pussycats instead. We shall defer that argument to Chapter 8.

Just because the emphasis has been on the animal – rather than on the ecological relationship itself – ecological research has been very time-consuming. A sound estimate of year-to-year variation in an animal's circumstances requires at least five years' observations. That is why ecologists have generally assumed that no serious investigation can take less than five years. Such being the general opinion, it is no surprise to find that ecological investigations have indeed taken five years or more. This is one main reason why there are so few valid generalizations in ecology: the time needed to collect enough case-histories has exceeded the working life of the ecologist. Lack (1954, 1966) is one of the few ecologists who has managed to deduce broad principles from a sufficient quantity of hard evidence. But the basic components of an ecological relationship remain the same from year to year: the numbers of animals may vary, but their physiological requirements, and their repertoire of behaviour, remain unchanged. Therefore,

4

once we shift our attention from the animals themselves to their relationships, we can complete an investigation in as little time–perhaps only one or two years–as may be needed to survey all the component parts of a given relationship. We shall return to this point later. But it means that we can accumulate enough case-histories to make valid comparisons and generalizations.

There is nothing new in this argument. Holling (1966) pioneered the study of predator–prey relationships in the laboratory, using the species most convenient for his purpose. In this book, we shall extend Holling's methods to suit conditions in the field. Field studies cannot offer the elegance of detail which Holling achieved in the laboratory; but in exchange we get far greater realism in each individual study and far greater confidence in generalizations made by comparing different studies (Chapter 8). An ecological relationship, observed in the laboratory, can and does differ so much from the same relationship in the field that conclusions drawn solely from laboratory work are quite misleading (Chapter 4). Therefore, this book will concentrate on field studies. This does not mean that laboratory work is useless, but that it can only be an adjunct to field work. Only in the field can we study an ecological relationship, certain that we see its full complexity. It may be objected that, only too often, technical difficulties prevent the observation of all the components of some relationship in the field. True enough, the ecologist must at present walk a very narrow path between the trivial (e.g. keeping beetles in bottles – the well-known *Tribolium* experiments will be mentioned later in this chapter) and the impracticable (e.g. investigating the workings of a large ecosystem). But these problems can be overcome, if we choose appropriate and tractable species to study (Chapter 2).

We shall follow Dr Holling's lead in another matter. The study of an ecological relationship should embrace all its component parts. But once those component parts have been studied, how can they be assembled into a coherent whole? The only method available is the simulation model, i.e. a set of mathematical equations which are solved by numerical computation. Such a model, which mimics the component biological processes in some detail, in no way resembles the statistical regression 'model' which underlies, for example, k-factor analysis. By mathematical standards, a simulation model is a clumsy tool. But there is no other tool to hand, since the mathematical equations, if at all realistic, are far too complicated to be solved by analytic methods. A series of such models will appear in later chapters. These models are merely tools. They summarize the biological information about the case in question. If they reveal nothing about the way the component parts fit together to make the whole relationship, they are useless. Purely theoretical models, based on no real data at all, are therefore fatuous (except when used to explore theoretical problems arising from concrete cases). To avoid misunderstandings, the simulation model should preferably be put together by the same people who collect the field data. As yet, few people can do both jobs. As a second best, the biologist may collaborate with a mathematician. Both must accept that the biology takes precedence over the mathematics. In our experience, such collaboration is perfectly possible, but it must be far closer than the casual collaboration between, say, a biologist and a consulting statistician. Each partner should understand every aspect of the other's work, and participate in it, so that the distinction between biology and mathematics disappears. Only in this way will the biologist lose his fear of mathematics and the mathematician his incomprehension of practical field work. For it is only the field worker who can appreciate the full difficulty and complexity of ecological research; most problems of laboratory work, or of analysis, are relatively simple.

The object of any ecological research is to understand how the ecological mechanisms work in any particular case, to predict the effects of human interventions, or to seek broader generalizations (Chapter 8). Therefore, the simulation model is not an end in itself, and we are certainly not saying that every ecological investigation must include one. But the model does promote a further change of emphasis. In the past, a population ecologist has taken a number of samples through the season and has concentrated his attention on the numbers of animals in those samples. He has been in the same position as a photographer with a series of still pictures. The simulation model is more akin to cinematography. It has to represent, and explain, the changes in numbers from one sample to the next, in terms of the processes which determine those changes. There is a change of emphasis from population statics to true population dynamics, and from mere changes in numbers to the underlying mechanisms.

Such are the considerations which have prompted our approach to ecological research. We do not insist that this approach is superior to others, or that our methods are incapable of improvement. In a subject as backward as ecology today, there is room for any number of different attacks. The subject certainly has its fair share of short-cut fancies. It has suffered from stultifying arguments about density-dependence, erroneous theories of predator–prey oscillations, circular arguments about niches and now a craze for electrophoresis genetics and for r- and K-selection. None of these topics is entirely empty, but each has become over-inflated, and therefore (if we are right) will in time collapse. Only one current approach is, we submit, actually deleterious. It is an offshoot of the work of MacArthur, who, rightly recognizing the danger of becoming lost in detail, set out to search for generalizations at a high level of abstraction. MacArthur's attempt was very worthwhile: how successful it was must be a matter of opinion: but his work has spawned a purely mathematico-theoretical school, whose practitioners pay little attention to real animals and plants. (The mathematics involved is, by mathematical standards, entirely trivial.) It is indeed regrettable that students of ecology should be encouraged to shun contact with animals and plants in the belief that algebraic formulae can somehow replace them.

At first sight, our distrust of mathematical theories, and of studies made purely in the laboratory, may appear extreme.

Introduction

There are two different problems here. There is the problem of the purely theoretical worker, mentioned in the previous paragraph, and there is the problem of the laboratory worker who never ventures out into the field. Just how serious these problems are may be seen (for example) in the book edited by Usher and Williamson (1974). Of the papers in that book, four refer at least peripherally to field data, three more use laboratory data only and five use no data at all! By contrast, Holling (1973), writing on the same subject, repeatedly appeals to examples from the real world. Our argument is that theoretical or laboratory results are too unrealistic to be trusted until they have been tested in the field. For example, not a single animal population has yet been discovered which consistently obeys the Lotka–Volterra equations, even approximately. Yet the theoreticians constantly invoke those equations: first, because the equations are fairly tractable mathematically, and secondly, because no *realistic* set of equations has yet been found which describes the dynamics of animal populations in general. Such equations, if they exist at all, can be discovered only in the field: and until they *have* been discovered, we see no point in pursuing purely fictitious alternatives. The use of Lotka–Volterra equations, in fact, imposes on the theory a uniformity which does not exist in nature. Again, there has been much theoretical speculation on the 'stability' of predator–prey relationships, but the very first such relationship to be examined, in detail, in the field flouts all existing theories (Chapter 4). We doubt whether non-mathematical ecologists always appreciate how critically the results of theoretical work depend on the biological assumptions, either explicit or implicit, which the equations embody. And we are quite sure that most mathematicians, physicists or engineers who work on biological problems never realize how severely an ignorance of biology – and especially a lack of everyday contact with the animals and plants – handicaps their work.

The second problem is that of ecological studies done solely in the laboratory. Here again, there are sufficient examples to show that such studies are not to be trusted until they have been tested in the field. Carl (1970) has found that *Tribolium confusum* Duval, kept in milk bottles but given the chance to escape by walking out along a piece of string, never approaches the population densities of the classical *Tribolium* experiments, which therefore portray the behaviour of animals forcibly kept in prison. The results of those experiments are therefore quite unrealistic. If the predator–prey relationship of Chapter 4 was studied in the laboratory at constant temperature (and laboratory predator–prey studies usually *are* done at constant temperature), the overriding effect of temperature changes in the field would be completely overlooked. Yet the effect of temperature dominates the whole relationship. The danger that laboratory work will miss 'some all-important factor is therefore acute. We can study an ecological relationship in the laboratory and deduce a 'complete' description of its workings, while remaining blithely unaware that we have missed the real point. This does not mean that laboratory work is useless. On the contrary, every field study in this book relies to some extent on information collected in the laboratory, and in one case (Chapter 4) the whole study was necessarily done first in the laboratory before it could be taken out into the field. Until recently, it was possible to argue that certain kinds of ecological relationship are too difficult to study in the field, and can only be tackled in the laboratory. That argument, if true, would mean that ecology is a technically impossible subject. We are glad to say that the argument is not true.

It may be objected that our distrust of speculative theories, and of purely laboratory studies, flies in the face of some current philosophies of science. In any kind of scientific work, so we are told, scientists should erect theories and hypotheses, and then test them experimentally (see Appendix). We have no quarrel with that recipe – although whether successful scientists always follow it is another matter. Certainly, we must choose the questions to be asked with great care. The trouble is that so many ecological theories are not tested at all, or only in the laboratory. How many current ecological theories are actually worth testing must be a matter of opinion: but there is no sense in producing theories, if they are not to be tested in the field. Some theoreticians argue that it is up to the field workers to test their theories for them. We think that any distinction between theoretician and experimental worker, in ecology, is entirely premature. In mature sciences like physics and chemistry, that distinction is unavoidable. In a young science like ecology (where techniques of both theory and experiment are still very elementary), such a distinction is not only unnecessary, but positively harmful, because of the mutual incomprehension that inevitably arises between mathematician and biologist (Chapter 8).

There is absolutely no reason why ecological theorists should not test their own theories in the field: and every field ecologist can think of excellent questions, or hypotheses, for himself, without the help of theoreticians. It might be objected that the poor showing of ecological research over the past fifty years demonstrates that field ecologists have not been asking the right questions. There is much to be said for that argument, in the sense that many of the questions that have been asked, although admirable in their own way, could not be answered with the technical facilities available. But it is the field ecologist who best knows the limitations of his own techniques; we see no evidence that the questions currently posed by theoreticians are any more tractable. Our attitude contains no element of antipathy to theory as such, for we shall use well-established (and, we hope, fairly realistic) genetical theory in Chapter 3. We simply distrust theory done for theory's sake. It is no mathematical or theoretical difficulty that holds us up in ecology, but our sheer ignorance of events in the field. When that ignorance has been dispelled, ecology will need its Keynes: but first we must consult the animals and plants. This book describes one way to do it. The last three paragraphs have been written in response to heavy criticism, and we apologize to any field ecologist to whom these arguments are obvious.

Our distrust of speculative theories, and of laboratory

studies that are never taken into the field, has one unfortunate consequence. If this book were about simulation models in ecology, we could discuss a wide range of cases, either theoretical or based on laboratory work. But we are concerned with realistic studies of natural ecological relationships, using simulation models (where necessary) as a tool: and as Streifer (1974) shows, there are precious few studies available – but enough for our purposes. Therefore, unavoidably, the following chapters will rely heavily on our own work, although we shall certainly invoke other examples where relevant. This regrettable situation is only temporary, for several more field studies along these lines are in progress in various parts of the world. Had we known of it, we could have used one of the studies listed by Ruesink (1976); the others are not detailed enough, or have not been tested in the field.

Many published cases cannot be used because some vital piece of information is missing. Purely as an example: Dempster (1971) has made a magnificent study of the cinnabar moth *Tyria jacobaeae* L. and its parasite *Apanteles popularis* Hal., but that work cannot be used to illustrate the parasite–host relationship because the level of hyperparasitism was not recorded. This does not, of course, invalidate Dempster's work for its original purpose; and there are plenty of holes in our own work too! (Chapter 10). Current work on crop physiology (e.g. Evans 1975), on animal husbandry (e.g. Rice *et al.* 1974) and on human demography (e.g. Coale 1972) uses methods quite similar to those in this book, but except in certain cases mentioned in Chapter 5, the results are not relevant to the ecological problems discussed here. Nor can we invoke the theory of systems analysis, because the ecological systems investigated here are decidedly non-linear. Our choice of methods, and of examples, is dictated by the need for biological realism. We hope to show that realistic studies of ecological relationships can be made in the field, and tested for completeness.

2 POPULATION DYNAMICS

For reasons given in Chapter 1, this book will concentrate not on species, but on relationships: and for purely technical reasons, it will concentrate on relationships between populations. The larger problems of whole ecosystems are deferred to Chapter 8. The basic tool for population studies is the life-table, i.e. a table of the birth- and survival-rates experienced by each age-class of the population. This chapter discusses the construction of variable life-tables, whose birth- and survival-rates change with time in a realistic way. Later chapters will study the various kinds of ecological relationship which link together pairs of populations, and which therefore link together the two corresponding life-tables. Since rather few studies have so far been made, we shall constantly refer to rather few case-histories; but these few span the whole range of possible relationships. A detailed, step-by-step analysis of one such case-history appears in Part 2.

Choice of species

The emphasis on relationships means that we can choose to work on whatever species may be technically most convenient. Species which lend themselves to one kind of study may be quite unsuited to another. But every population study requires that, so far as possible:

(1) The natural history of each species involved, should be well known.

(2) All stages should be easy to observe and sample, and have clearly defined sampling units (Chapter 7).

(3) Different age-groups and morphs, e.g. sexes, should be readily distinguishable, to permit the construction of life-tables.

(4) The animals should be inexpensive to rear and easy to handle in the laboratory.

(5) Generation time should be no more than a year, and preferably much less: otherwise, it will be the ecologist who expires first.

In addition, each particular type of study has its own requirements. The predator–prey studies of Chapter 4 require that the predation process can be observed in the field: that, for simplicity's sake, the predator should be restricted to one main source of food during the period of study: and that the predator–prey relationship should preferably extend over a wide geographical range, to permit comparisons of different climates and lengths of season. By contrast, plant–herbivore studies require that the plant should be small enough for experimental manipulation and should have a short life-cycle: that individual plants should form recognizable, discrete units: and that the rates of herbivore attack on different parts of the plant should be measurable. The reasons for these requirements appear in Chapter 5. Studies of movement (Chapter 6) are even more demanding. It must be possible to track the movements of individual animals: all the animals should be conspicuous and readily identifiable: we must know what the animals are searching for (or avoiding) and be able to measure their success: the animals must not behave differently because of our presence: and we should, if possible, be able to measure both local and long-distance movements.

Some of these requirements are obviously restrictive, and may have to be relaxed. We can hardly expect any one species to satisfy them perfectly. The species which most nearly satisfy the requirements are found among the arthropods, and in particular, among the insects. Consequently, the case-histories in this book will all concern insects and their host plants. We shall argue in Chapter 8 that the choice of suitable species is much wider than it appears to be at first sight. Meanwhile, certain species of aphid and their natural enemies have proved to be convenient for work on predator–prey relationships. The

Population dynamics

aphids satisfy all five basic requirements for population studies. Many species of aphid attack only one species of host plant, and the plant itself forms a natural sampling unit (Chapter 7). Aphids appear fairly regularly from year to year; they do not confront the ecologist with the technical problems of shifts from extreme rarity to great abundance. Of the plants and insects so far used in plant–herbivore studies, cotton and its insect pests have proved the most suitable. The medium size and simple growth-pattern of cotton are ideal for physiological analysis; and insect damage is easily measured, since cotton is attacked mainly by chewing, rather than sucking or mining, insects. For the study of animal movement, certain species of butterfly are very suitable. The females search only for nectar and for host plants on which to lay eggs, and the eggs laid are a record of the female's immediate success in finding host plants. Since the caterpillars satisfy the basic requirements for population studies, it is possible to study the effects of the female's movement pattern on the subsequent dynamics of the population (Chapter 6).

The choice of insects – or of arthropods generally – as subjects for ecological study, has given an unexpected bonus. We mentioned in Chapter 1 that the emphasis has changed from population statics to true population dynamics. This obviously invokes questions of timing: and as we shall see, timing (development rate) and numbers (fecundity) are intimately linked. Because the rate of development of insects depends on ambient temperature, their timing varies – and can be varied experimentally too – with temperature, which of course is not true of homeotherms. It is therefore much easier to study the effects of timing with insects than with mammals or birds.

A population model is merely a glorified life-table. Starting with any specified number and age-distribution of animals, the birth- and survival-rates listed in the life-table will predict the subsequent dynamics of the population. If different, recognizable categories of animal (e.g. male and female) experience sharply different survival rates, those categories are accounted separately. Immigration and emigration, if significant, must be represented. For a population study, therefore, the ecologist's task is merely to specify the birth- and survival-rates, the numbers of immigrants and emigrants and the initial state of the population. If the experimentally derived birth- and survival-rates, and the initial numbers and age-distribution, are right, they *must* predict the correct population dynamics.

If the birth- and survival-rates in the life-table are constant, the future course of events may be predicted using purely analytic mathematical methods (e.g. Coale 1972). But in nature, birth- and survival-rates vary, not only with age of animal, but also with time. The mathematics then becomes intractable and we have to use computer simulation models to predict the population dynamics. A computer population model is therefore a 'variable life-table'.

To describe the observed population dynamics in one particular season, we need merely quote the appropriate birth- and survival-rates as they change with time. But, whether for scientific understanding or practical management, we need to know how those rates are affected by changing conditions, both intrinsic and external to the population. We want to understand the biological mechanisms which specify what the rates shall be. It then becomes possible to predict the effects of changes imposed on the population, and to predict what would happen if the animals themselves did something different (Chapter 3). Thus a crude, purely descriptive model may quote the birth- and survival-rates as functions of time alone, but a rich, predictive model must simulate the biological mechanisms which determine those rates. The more precise the biological description, the better understanding we have, and the wider the range of circumstances for which the model gives accurate predictions.

Physiological time-scales

If the life-table, or population model, is to predict the population dynamics correctly, it must work on the correct

Population dynamics

time-scale. In the case of homeotherms, the correct time-scale is, clearly, calendar time. But an insect's rate of development and growth depends on temperature, as well as on factors such as the species or age of host-plant. If we base an insect population model on calendar time, we must allow for the effect of temperature. But it is much simpler to base the model on the insect's own 'physiological' time-scale, which is a combination of calendar time and temperature.

Fig. 2.1 shows the usual relationship between an insect's rate of development and temperature. Below a threshold temperature, there is no development. Over the intermediate range of temperatures which the insect normally experiences in the field, the rate of development increases linearly with temperature. Why this should be is a mystery, since rates of enzyme action (which are presumably basic to development) usually increase exponentially, not linearly, with temperature.

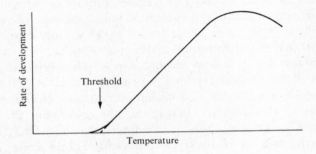

Fig. 2.1 Rate of insect development as a function of temperature.

At unusually high temperatures, the rate of development declines, but this rarely happens in the field: the temperature requirements of different species and populations are adjusted to suit the local temperature regimes. Thus the rate of development is directly proportional to the ambient temperature, measured above the threshold temperature. The total amount of development during any given time period is proportional to the length of time, multiplied by the temperature above the threshold. On this 'physiological time-scale' of day–degrees, development proceeds at a constant rate, whatever the actual temperature. Hughes (1963) first used the physiological time-scale in this context.

Campbell *et al.* (1974) describe physiological time-scales in detail, and show how they are estimated empirically. To make an insect population model on a physiological, rather than on the calendar, time-scale greatly simplifies its construction: so all the models used in this book use physiological time-scales. Where a model simulates the ecological relationship between two animals with sharply different physiological time-scales, it must use both at once (Gutierrez, Denton *et al.* 1974).

The fact that insects operate on a time-scale, not of days, but of day–degrees, raises an important point of philosophy. For insects at any rate, it is not *in principle* possible to predict that 'the population will increase by so many in the next week', but only that 'it will increase by so many in the next hundred day–degrees'. We must then wait to see how long that physiological time-period takes in calendar time. It may take many days at low temperatures, and fewer at higher temperatures. For insects, it will *never* be possible to predict field events in calendar time until temperatures can be forecast very accurately.

Since field samples are taken in calendar time, the physiological time-scale must still be matched against calendar time. We do this with a computer program which fits sine curves to successive pairs of daily maximum and minimum temperatures recorded in the field, and calculates the corresponding increment of physiological time. Each calendar day is converted to the corresponding number of day–degrees, starting at some arbitrary time-origin (just as calendar time starts at the arbitrary origin of January 1st). In this way, the daily temperatures throughout the season are converted to physiological time. This method was first used by Arnold (1960) in horticulture and by Morris and Bennett (1967) in

Population dynamics

entomology: the computer algorithm is listed by Frazer and Gilbert (1976). Although the sine curve only approximates the irregular variation of temperature through the day, the method gives a remarkably good approximation to the true temperature summation obtained by numerical integration of a continuous temperature record: the discrepancy, over a period of several days or longer, is usually less than 2%. A continuous temperature record therefore offers no advantage over records of daily maxima and minima only. The most serious inaccuracies arise not from the method, but from discrepancies between the temperatures recorded by instruments and those actually experienced by the insects in their microclimate.

Some general considerations

Before we begin to collect the biological data, we must consider several questions which apply to all ecological studies, whether or not they use simulation models. The first concerns the amount of biological detail required. Each ecological relationship is made up of numerous components which could be studied in broad outline, or in endless detail. There is only one rule to decide how much detail is actually required: each component process must be represented in sufficient detail, so that any additional variation which actually occurs will not seriously affect the biological answers finally obtained. But it is quite impracticable to include all possible details just to make sure that they do not affect the answer. A simulation model is therefore bound to be subjective: it includes as much detail as the ecologist judges to be necessary. That is true, not just of simulation models, but of all ecological investigations; the great virtue of models is that they oblige us to specify *every* component of the relationship under study, even if only in broad outline. The content of a model must evidently depend on the biological questions which it is expected to answer. If we are studying the relationship between predator A and its prey, the behaviour of A, being of primary interest, must be represented in detail. But if another predator B simultaneously attacks the same prey, it may be good enough to represent the effect of B as a simple mortality factor applied to the numbers of prey. As a general rule, therefore, the more central to the question under study some particular component or process may be, the greater the amount of detail it requires. The model itself may dictate how much detail is required, for if the model is too superficial, it will not reproduce the field observations at all (Chapter 4).

To illustrate this very important problem of the necessary level of detail, we shall consider the estimation of the lengths of time spent in successive instars by some species of insect. Where the generations are discrete (not overlapping in time), this may be attempted in the field using a calendar time-scale (e.g. Manly 1974). Successive field samples, taken during the course of one generation, show a 'wave': the earliest samples contain individuals in the earliest instars, while later samples contain progressively older individuals. Mortality will cause the absolute numbers to decline from sample to sample. In theory, therefore, it is possible to estimate, simultaneously, both the mortality rates and the lengths of time spent in each successive instar. But the method is statistically inaccurate, because it has to disentangle the twin effects of timing and mortality; more importantly, it is biologically unrealistic because it uses calendar time instead of physiological time. So the results are biased by changes in temperature, and cannot be extrapolated to quite different temperatures. It is far preferable to estimate the instar-times directly, by growing individuals at several different constant temperatures in the laboratory and observing the lengths of time spent in each instar. This gives accurate, independent estimates of instar-times on the physiological time-scale. The field samples may then be used to estimate mortality rates, and the estimates will be far more accurate than before, because the uncertainties surrounding the estimation of the instar-times will have disappeared. This is therefore a case where the extra effort is well repaid, not merely by improved accuracy, but by a wider range of applicability, *viz.* to the full range of temperatures experienced in the field.

At the other extreme, Stinner, Gutierrez and Butler (1974) have pointed out that where rates of insect development are not strictly linear functions of temperature, simple physiological time-scales do not give perfectly accurate results. We have yet to encounter a situation where this is a serious problem *in the field*: so the extra accuracy, and applicability, gained by an increase in detail is in this case unimportant. For example, Gilbert and Gutierrez (1973) found that the generation times observed in the field and throughout the season coincided exactly with those predicted by the simple physiological time-scale estimated in the laboratory. The same has been true of every case so far studied, involving insects with discrete generations. On the other hand, where temperature requirements vary from place to place (Campbell *et al.* 1974) or from year to year (Morris 1971), corresponding changes in the physiological time-scale must be considered.

The technical problems of making simulation models in general will not be discussed here (but see Part 2). Although important, they are outweighed by the biological and sampling problems posed by ecological work. When studying the behaviour of individual animals, we usually use stochastic models working on a continuous time-scale (Holling 1965, and Chapters 4 and 6). For population studies, we use deterministic models working in discrete time-steps. (The very important choice of an appropriate time-step is discussed in Chapter 9.) The distinction between stochastic and deterministic is, briefly, as follows. Suppose that a butterfly lays, on average, 80 eggs. Then the deterministic model assumes that every butterfly lays precisely 80 eggs. At each successive time-step, it applies the average birth- and survival-rates to the total numbers of animals in each age-class. For any specified set of conditions, the deterministic model need be run only once on the computer, to generate one average answer. The stochastic model takes the more reasonable view that different butterflies will lay different numbers of eggs. It incorporates the appropriate amounts of biological variation to generate not one answer, but a whole distribution of possible answers. It therefore demands more biological information – e.g., the distribution of numbers of eggs, not just the average number 80 – and gives correspondingly more information in return. But it requires far more computer time, because it must be run on the computer not once but many times, to generate a whole set of possible answers.

The behaviour of individual animals is essentially stochastic. It consists of a series of events, such as the laying of individual eggs or the capture of individual prey. The probability that any event shall, or shall not, occur at any specified time depends on biological factors such as predator hunger and prey size. If the event does in fact occur, it alters the probability of the next event; for example, when a predator catches and eats a prey, it becomes less hungry and therefore less likely to catch another prey. The mathematical equations describing individual behaviour, if at all realistic, must be solved numerically, treating the series of events as a stochastic process. For technical reasons, a deterministic treatment is rarely possible. Two cases of this kind are described in Chapter 11.

Ideally, population studies would be treated stochastically too, to give a whole range of possible answers. But that is usually not feasible, for two reasons already mentioned: lack of biological information, and the exorbitant amount of computer time which realistic stochastic models of complex population processes require. So we use a deterministic version which gives an average answer. It is admittedly possible that a deterministic model, incorporating non-linear components, might give an answer far removed from the average answer of the corresponding stochastic model. To this there are three, inadequate, replies. First, the amount of stochastic variation occurring in the field, and affecting each step of each component of the model, is generally unknown – it is difficult enough to amass the biological information required to make a realistic deterministic model. Secondly, when Gilbert and

Population dynamics

Hughes (1971) added the minimum theoretical amount of stochastic variation to a realistic population model, no great discrepancy appeared between the deterministic and the average stochastic answers. Nor is one likely to arise, except at very low population densities. Thirdly, differences between replicate experimental populations are surprisingly small (Frazer and Gilbert 1976). But a deterministic model gives no estimate of the variations in numbers that may reasonably be attributed to 'chance', and this is a major stumbling-block for validation of the model.

Validation

Once a simulation model has been made, the question at once arises: How much does the model truly reflect reality, and how much is it a figment of the ecologist's imagination? The same question arises for all ecological results, whether expressed as simulation models or not. We therefore have to decide whether a given population model is valid at all, and if so, over what range of circumstances.

Clearly, if a population model is to be 'valid', it must reproduce the field data correctly. It is sometimes argued that a model may be 'explanatory', describing a considerable part of the underlying biological machinery, without predicting the correct answer. And so it may: but such a model evidently contains a serious error somewhere, and until that error has been located, we can have no confidence in any part of the model which has not been checked independently. This takes us back to the essential requirement for biological realism, discussed in Chapter 1. It is quite true that 'explanatory' models which do not predict the field data correctly arise as intermediate steps in the construction of a realistic, valid model: but they are only intermediate steps, and valuable only because they identify the sources of error (Chapters 9 and 10). We can have no confidence in a model, unless it reproduces the field data correctly. Our confidence is increased if the model correctly predicts not just the numbers of each species present throughout the season, but a wide range of concomitant variables such as age-distributions, morph frequencies etc. As mentioned above, a deterministic model does not estimate 'residual' variances, and so the comparison between observation and prediction cannot be statistically rigorous, unless independent replicated data have been collected in the field. Usually we use experience to judge whether the agreement between prediction and observation is reasonable (but see Chapter 7).

But a model which merely reproduces the data is valueless. It is only too easy to construct purely empirical mathematical expressions which reproduce a given set of data, but which cannot predict how the populations will react to altered circumstances. Therefore, we must be reasonably confident that the model simulates the true biological mechanisms well enough to predict population behaviour over the full range of circumstances which the population normally encounters. At present, such confidence is very much a matter of biological judgement – the biology built into the model must 'feel right'. Clearly, the model will begin to go wrong when it begins to extrapolate any one of its component mechanisms unreasonably far beyond the range of the data used to estimate that mechanism. It is a simple matter to apply checks against unreasonable extrapolation, either within the computer program, or by inspection. But the model will also go wrong when some biological mechanism, not represented in the model at all, begins to have a significant effect in the field. There is no final solution to that problem, and it underlines the importance of choosing species whose behaviour may be directly observed in the field (Chapter 1).

It is therefore impossible to specify precisely the limits of validity of a population model. Those who argue against the use of simulation models at all, for that reason, should reflect that the same argument applies to all ecological work. Moreover, this is not a very serious problem in practice. For example, the pattern of growth of kale plants, on which Hughes (1963) observed the dynamics of ·cabbage aphid

Population dynamics

(*Brevicoryne brassicae* (L.)) populations, is similar from season to season. So the simulation model, which embodies an average pattern of plant growth, is trustworthy for every season in S.E. Australia, but can give no reliable insight into aphid population dynamics on a different host plant or in a different area. In some cases, it is possible to make an independent test of the validity of a population model by invoking the theory of natural selection. This test is introduced in Chapter 3. Another way of testing is to verify the model's predictions experimentally (Chapter 7).

3 A CRITERION OF POPULATION SUCCESS

For reasons stated in Chapter 2, every population model must be, to some extent, subjective. Moreover, any population model might be seriously incomplete: while reproducing the field data well enough, the model might completely overlook some important component of the ecological relationship, or treat it as constant when it is, in fact, variable. It is therefore very desirable to have some independent test that the model is valid. Ideally, all component parts of the model would be estimated quite independently of the population data, and used to predict the course of population events for comparison with that actually observed. In the present state of the art, that is asking rather a lot; some components must often be estimated from the population data themselves (cf. Part 2), in which case the independent comparison between prediction and observation is lost. But sometimes we can appeal to theory. If natural selection has maximized some criterion of population success, the model ought to show the same maximum: in other words, the numerical value of the criterion, as predicted by the model, should decline when any parameter of the model is either increased or decreased. For if not, the model implies that the animals could do better if they did something different. What, then, is the right criterion to use? The question is answered by the genetical theory of Fisher (1930). In this chapter, we shall apply that theory to our ecological purposes.

Fisher's principle of maximal 'fitness'
Fisher shows that natural selection tends to maximize the 'fitness' of any interbreeding population. 'Fitness' in this context is the average, or expected, number of offspring

contributed by each individual to the succeeding generation. 'Fitness' is maximized, not for any individual, but for the population as a whole. The theory is the same, whether generations are discrete or overlapping. It then becomes a question of applying the theory to each particular case-history.

In the simplest case, where animals survive to maturity, reproduce at once, and then die, 'fitness' equals the survival rate multiplied by the fecundity. So the genes controlling any phenotypic character–perhaps the length of the animal's body, or the fecundity itself–are selected to maximize the expression (survival to reproductive age × fecundity). If those genes affect survival but not fecundity, they are accordingly selected to maximize that survival. If pleiotropic genes affect two or more phenotypic characters at once, those characters will be co-adjusted so that they mutually maximize population 'fitness'. Obviously, if the 'fitness' exceeds one, more animals will appear in each generation than in the previous one, i.e. the population size will increase until it is arrested by density-dependent ecological changes: but this ecological consideration does not affect the genetical argument, that natural selection confers on the population that genetical constitution which, compared with other possible genetical constitutions, maximizes population 'fitness'. The ecological conditions specify the working limitations within which natural selection has to act: and natural selection then determines the most suitable genetical constitution for the population. This entire argument supersedes the old opinion, still sometimes encountered (e.g. Birdsell 1972), that the fecundity of each species is somehow adjusted to counterbalance the mortality which that species unavoidably suffers.

The simple expression for 'fitness', i.e. survival to reproductive age × fecundity, must be broadened when animals experience a long reproductive period, or when post-reproductive animals influence the survival of their progeny. This does not affect the principle that 'fitness' is maximized. But during periods of population increase or decrease, the more complicated idea of 'reproductive value' must be substituted for 'fitness' (Fisher 1930). Therefore, where a population characteristically goes through an ecological cycle lasting several generations, its 'fitness' will be maximized over the whole cycle, but not necessarily in each generation. And in some hypothetical genetical situations, 'fitness' is not precisely maximized (Moran 1962), although it is not known whether such genetical situations actually occur. Thus, it is always possible that the genetical mechanisms are themselves adapted to secure the optimization, not precisely of 'fitness', but of some other characteristic.

Despite these reservations, it remains broadly true that any changes in population parameters, away from the values actually observed, should cause population 'fitness' to decline; and so any valid simulation model of the population dynamics must show the same effect. Obviously, if the simulation model is to predict 'fitness' over a whole generation (or ecological cycle), it must reproduce the population dynamics throughout that period. Very often, a simulation model covers only part of one generation. In that case, it can be tested against the principle of maximum 'fitness' only if that principle can be applied to the period represented in the model. Sometimes it can, sometimes not. In the rest of this chapter, we shall examine various applications of the principle.

Particular applications of Fisher's principle

The simplest case arises when animals survive to maturity, breed once and die. For example, most species of salmon spawn only once. Then 'fitness' is the survival rate from egg to adult, multiplied by the fecundity. (Instead of starting at the egg stage, we could start counting at any other stage of the life-cycle, since the overall survival rate throughout one complete cycle must be the same.) It is reasonable to suppose that many phenotypic characters, e.g. the light-reflecting properties of fish scales, affect survival but not fecundity – in which case, they will be selected to maximize survival only. It is often conjectured that, within the observed range of fecundities, the fecundity of an individual fish does not affect the survival of its progeny; or more precisely, the genes which control individual fecundity do not also affect individual survival. In that case, natural selection will favour ever-increasing fecundity, up to a point where some other mechanism begins to act. This might be some physiological limitation on the adult fish, e.g. food intake; or it might be that increased fecundity implies smaller eggs, and therefore reduced survival of those eggs. Evidently we could not expect a simulation model of the population dynamics to show that the observed fecundity is optimal unless the model includes the effect of the limiting mechanism, whatever it may be. Yet a simulation model, deficient in that respect, might still be perfectly capable of predicting (say) the effect of imposing some fishing regime on the population. Thus the fact that a model fails the 'maximum fitness' test does not necessarily invalidate it for other purposes.

Let us next consider the cases where parents care for their offspring during a nursery period, and then release them into the population at large. The more offspring one parent produces, the less parental care can be devoted to each, and so the smaller the chance of survival of each offspring. In other words, the genes which control fecundity also affect survival of the progeny, up to the end of the period of parental care, but presumably not thereafter. The fecundity will as usual be selected to maximize population 'fitness', and in such cases, this is equivalent to maximizing the average number of offspring per parent which survive to the end of the period of parental care. This is the principle adopted by Lack (1954). It will not be correct in cases where genetic variations in family size affect survival of the offspring *after* the period of parental care. Such cases might arise when parental care is equally divided among all the progeny, so that the progeny in a large family are relatively small and weak at the end of the period of parental care. That possibility is largely eliminated in those species of bird which feed the strongest chick in the nest first, the next strongest second, and so on. Where a parent bird raises several consecutive families, Lack's principle will apply to the total number of surviving offspring per parent, but need not apply to the numbers of surviving offspring in one family. For if the parental care expended on a large family exhausts the parent bird and so reduces its chances of surviving to breed again, the average size of each family may be reduced accordingly (cf. Charnov and Krebs 1974). These considerations apart, Lack's principle demands knowledge of biological events during the period of parental care only, not during the whole life-cycle.

The next case, that of *Masonaphis maxima*, is more complex. Here the progeny of fundatrix aphids go through a population cycle consisting of several parthenogenetic generations, ending with a sexual generation which produces the overwintering eggs from which the next year's fundatrices emerge. Every phenotypic character will be selected to maximize population 'fitness' which in this case is the average number of fundatrix descendants, in the following year, per individual fundatrix in this year. The simulation model (Chapter 9) does not cover the periods of egglaying and winter survival, and so cannot predict this total measure of 'fitness': but we can substitute a partial measure, namely the average number of sexual individuals produced per fundatrix throughout the season. Every phenotypic character x will be selected to maximize that partial measure of 'fitness', provided that x (or strictly speaking, the genes which control x) does not affect the number of eggs laid per sexual female, or the individual chances of overwinter survival. Gilbert and Gutierrez (1973) successfully tested the simulation model, using that partial measure of 'fitness'.

When the character x is chosen to be the fecundity of parthenogenetic aphids, a rather peculiar situation arises, intermediate between the fish and bird cases which we have just discussed. A group of n fundatrices colonize a plant, and their progeny subsequently compete for the food which that plant supplies. So the number of progeny x produced by each fundatrix is controlled by her own genotype, but the subsequent survival rate z of her progeny depends on the total number of offspring produced by all the fundatrices on the plant, i.e. on the genotypes of all fundatrices in the group. A fairly involved algebraic argument shows that maximization of 'fitness' then entails the maximization of

$$V \log (x) + V_{gp} \log (z), \tag{1}$$

where V is the genetic variance of individual fecundity x, and V_{gp} is the between-group genetic variance of the mean fecundity x of the aphids in each group. This result does not require that the number of fundatrices must be the same in every group. But if every group is founded by n unrelated fundatrices, $V_{gp} = V/n$, and maximizing expression (1) is equivalent to maximizing $xz^{1/n}$ (Gilbert and Gutierrez 1973). (In the bird case, $n = 1$: in the fish case, n is effectively infinite.) This is the familiar result that selection acting on groups of n unrelated individuals is only $1/n$ times as effective as selection of individuals. But if the individuals in the group are genetically related, V_{gp} exceeds V/n, and group selection is correspondingly more effective. This theory therefore includes the existing theories of group and kin selection (Williams 1971, Eberhard 1975) as special cases.

Applications of Fisher's principle to ecology

This chapter uses Fisher's theory to test, as far as possible, the realism and completeness of a population model. The 'maximum fitness' test was tried on a simulation model of the population dynamics of an insect parasite, *Diaeretiella rapae* (Gilbert and Hughes 1971). A dozen possible values, both greater and smaller than the observed value, were chosen for some vital parameter such as individual fecundity; the model was then run a dozen times, each time with a different chosen value for that parameter. This produces a curve which shows how population 'fitness', as predicted by the model, changes as the value of the parameter is changed. If the model is right, the curve should show a maximum at the true, observed, value of the parameter. The test confirmed that, according to the model, the parasite's vital parameters are adjusted to maximize its 'fitness'. The authors thought at the time that this result told them something about the parasite; only later did they realize that it was really a test of the simulation model. It was not possible to try the same test on the aphid, *Brevicoryne brassicae*, which the parasite attacks, because the aphid's relationship to its host plant had not been studied. Where, in another case, an aphid–host plant relationship had been studied, the test worked well (Gilbert and Gutierrez 1973). It did not work well on the parasite–aphid relationship in the same study, showing conclusively that our understanding of the parasite's population dynamics is less than complete (Chapter 10). It might be argued that the parasite is a recent arrival which has not yet adjusted to its new situation; but it is far more likely that the parasite is right, and we are wrong. The coccinellid–aphid study of Frazer and Gilbert (1976) could not be tested, because it covers only a small part of the coccinellid's life-cycle.

In the cases just mentioned, the observed maxima are sharp, i.e. the 'fitness' declines rapidly on either side of the optimal values of the parameters concerned. So we cannot accept Miller's (1974) assertion that, if a simulation model is biologically correct, it should be insensitive to changes in the values of its parameters. We agree with Taylor (1975) that it would be difficult to apply the test to an extremely migratory species such as *Aphis fabae* Scop., simply because the technical problems of comparing the 'reproductive values' of sessile wingless progeny, and of migratory winged progeny, are prohibitive. But we do not agree with Taylor, or for that matter with Gilbert and Hughes (1971), that animal populations – including clones of aphids – are geared to minimize their probabilities of extinction, rather than to maximize 'fitness'. The two criteria are different, although very closely correlated (which means, incidentally, that ecological 'resilience' (Holling 1973) is an automatic consequence of Fisher's theory: maximization of 'fitness' will make the population 'resilient' at the same time). It is true that extinction

A criterion of population success

is the ultimate evolutionary calamity, a fact which is reflected in the logarithmic terms of expression (1): but on the ecological time-scale, natural selection favours, not merely the survival of a population, but its increase too.

Jones (1976a) has used the test rather differently. If her descriptions of caterpillar searching behaviour are adequate, the model should show that the behaviour of the caterpillars is adjusted to maximize their survival, for the plant distribution which they normally encounter. Jones was therefore able to use her model to compare the suitabilities of different plant distributions observed in the field. This kind of argument obviously demands considerable discretion; for corresponding to almost any model, however erroneous, there will be some 'optimal' plant distribution. The danger is minimal when the criterion of success, viz. population 'fitness', is specified by considerations external to the model. Thus, in our experience, this theory not only offers a useful, independent test of population models, but sometimes helps to interpret their biological content.

But the theory does more than that. In a very broad sense, it tells the ecologist what questions to ask. For since natural selection acts to maximize population 'fitness', the ecologist's task is simply to observe what ecological mechanisms have been chosen to maximize population 'fitness', subject to the external conditions which restrict that choice.

4 PREDATOR-PREY RELATIONSHIPS

The next few chapters will examine particular kinds of ecological relationship. Here we shall consider predator–prey and insect host–parasite relationships. There is every reason to suppose (cf. Watt 1968) that pathogen–host relationships fall in the same category.

The object is to predict the effects of the predator–prey interaction on the survival and reproductive rates of both predator and prey in all circumstances normally encountered in the field. An insect parasite's reproductive rate, in general, equals the number of parasitized hosts, so that the effect on both parasite and host is specified by the survival rate of the hosts. Suppose that the prey (host) density is a, and the predator density is b. To predict the prey survival rate during a given time-period, Nicholson (1933) used the very crude theoretical expression $\exp(-sb)$. This assumes that the predator searches randomly, that it searches a constant area s during the time-interval and that it is insatiable. Hassell and May (1973) show how the quoted survival rate is deduced from these assumptions. Hughes and Gilbert (1968) used a different, but equally crude, expression, originally developed by Thompson (1924). It is derived as follows. If each predator requires k prey per time-period, the total demand for prey is kb. Since there are a prey, each prey individual expects to be attacked kb/a times. If predators search at random, the number of attacks per individual prey follows a Poisson distribution with mean kb/a, so that the survival rate (proportion of prey which escape attack) is the zero term of the distribution,

$$\exp(-kb/a). \tag{1}$$

We shall refer to this expression as the 'random search' survival rate, although it evidently depends on a further assumption, *viz.* that all predators have a constant demand for prey. It may be objected that one prey individual cannot be attacked twice, as the Poisson distribution implies. In the host–parasite case, the same individual can be, and is, attacked more than once. In the case of predation, expression (1) implies that the predators do not find all the prey·they need, unless kb/a is close to zero, in which case expression (1) is very nearly the same as

$$\frac{a - kb}{a} \tag{2}$$

Expression (2) means that where there is a great surplus of prey, the predators have no difficulty in finding them and simply help themselves to the number (kb) that they require. It is therefore reasonable to expect that wherever prey numbers greatly exceed the predators' requirements, expressions (1) and (2) will predict the survival rate reasonably well, given the correct value of k. But they go wrong when predators have difficulty in finding enough prey: expression (2) can actually become negative, while both expression (1) and Nicholson's version predict the appearance of those predator–prey oscillations which used to preoccupy the theoretical ecologists, and which have never been observed outside the laboratory.

These simple expressions for survival rate may be elaborated in two ways. The first is to pursue more sophisticated, but still theoretical, arguments. These have recently been surveyed by Royama (1971) and by Hassell and May (1973), and we shall refer to those papers as a summary of such theoretical work. Hassell and May refer to numerous studies of predation in the laboratory, and this brings us to the second approach – detailed study of actual predation processes. Holling (1965, 1966) pioneered that approach, and his work is still by far the outstanding exemplar. But it raises a number of difficulties. First, the study is made in the laboratory; it is not clear how far the results apply in the field. That very serious objection applies not only to Holling's work but to all laboratory studies

(Chapter 1). Secondly, Holling's realistic descriptions require very large numbers of parameters, which cannot be estimated in the field. Thirdly, realistic descriptions of individual predator and prey behaviour must still be translated into predation rates at the population level for all combinations of circumstances normally encountered in the field.

Hughes and Gilbert (1968) and Gilbert and Gutierrez (1973) used expression (1) to predict predation and parasitization rates in field studies. It reproduced very well the actual losses and gains – but always at low predator:prey ratios, so that predation had no very significant effect on the prey population. By contrast, Frazer and Gilbert (1976) found that expression (1) greatly overestimated the effect of predation by coccinellids, *Coccinella trifasciata* Mulsant, on a sparse population of pea aphids, *Acyrthosiphon pisum* (Harris). They were obliged to study the predation process in detail, and tie it into the population dynamics. The methodology is surveyed in Chapter 11. This is, so far as we know, the only case-history so far examined in this way, and so we shall have to base the following discussion on that one example. Frazer and Gilbert describe in detail how the necessary pieces of information were collected, and list computer programs which represent both the predation process and the consequent population dynamics: those programs therefore offer further examples, similar to that given in Chapters 9-10, of 'how the trick is done'.

The first problem mentioned above, that laboratory studies may not apply to field conditions, can be overcome only by studying the predation process in the field. It proved possible to do so. The predation process was first studied in the laboratory, along the lines developed by Holling. The result was a fairly complex description of the behaviour of both predators and prey, which satisfactorily predicted the predation rates observed in the laboratory. Some of the parameters in that description could be discarded – or rather, absorbed into other parameters – without seriously distorting the predicted predation rates. The remaining parameters fell into two categories: those whose values would remain the same in the field, and those that would obviously change. Parameters in the second category were then estimated again from a second study of the predation process, this time in the field.

This second study revealed, too, that the predation process in the field differed in several ways from the process observed in the laboratory. This procedure solved the second problem mentioned above, for the number of essential parameters to be estimated in the field was reduced to three – the average time which a hungry predator spends searching one plant when it catches no prey on that plant; the probability that, when a hungry predator searches one plant, it catches any given prey individual which is currently on that plant; and the average time spent on one plant when prey are caught. The third parameter varies according to the number and size of prey caught. It was then possible to predict the predation rate, in the field, at any given time. To do so, we have to know not only the predator and prey densities, but the prey age-distribution and the temperature as well. The third problem, of translating from the behavioural to the population level, was easily solved. The obvious solution would be to use the detailed stochastic model of the predation process (Chapter 11) as a subroutine of the population model, and so compute the survival rate *ab initio* for every new set of circumstances. But this demands quite exorbitant amounts of computer time. Instead, we use the predation model to compute survival rates for a whole set of different circumstances, covering the full range of conditions encountered in the field. To that set of survival rates we fit a 'response surface', i.e. an empirical algebraic formula which gives the correct value in every case. That formula is then used to compute survival rates in the population model.

In the coccinellid–aphid case, it proved quite easy to fit a response surface embodying all the four important factors. It is possible that, in future cases, it will be less easy to fit an over-all response-surface to predation rates affected by several different factors; in that case, the translation from individual predatory behaviour to population dynamics will be a serious technical problem, but one which can, if necessary, be overcome by interpolation from an extensive table of computed survival rates. Thus Frazer and Gilbert were able to take predation studies out into the field, and they were able to reconcile the predicted survival rates with the observed population dynamics of the prey.

This case illustrates the point, made in Chapter 2, that a particular level of realistic detail is essential if a population model is to reproduce the field observations at all. In this case, and in the movement studies of Chapter 6, work at the level of individual behaviour is vital to any understanding of the population dynamics. In particular, the variable of individual hunger, first invoked by Holling, not only controls the whole predation process, but reappears as an important factor in animal movement:

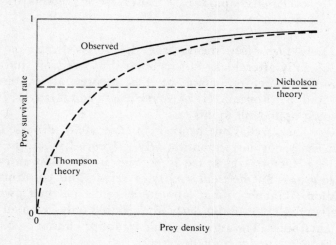

Fig. 4.1 Theoretical and observed rates of prey survival per unit time, as functions of prey density.

The differences between the theoretical expressions of Nicholson and Thompson, and the predation rate deduced from the field observations, may be seen in Figure 4.1, which shows all three predation rates for a fixed number of predators and varying numbers of prey. Nicholson assumes that the insatiable predators search a fixed proportion of the available area, and therefore catch a fixed proportion of the available prey, irrespective of prey density. Thompson assumes that, as prey density declines, the predators take an ever-increasing proportion, so that the survival rate sinks to zero and the prey become extinct. The true situation is intermediate. At high prey densities, the predators are quickly satiated; but at low prey density, they have not enough time to find all the prey they need, and the survival rate does not approach zero – some prey always survive. The comparison in Figure 4.1 is not exact, because the true survival rate varies according to the ambient temperature and the age-distribution of the prey, both of which factors the theoretical rates ignore.

The coccinellid–aphid case raises several points of very general interest.

(1) As previously mentioned, the survival rate is very significantly affected by factors other than predator and prey density. Therefore, none of the theoretical expressions surveyed by Royama (1971) or Hassell and May (1973) is remotely applicable to this case.

(2) The predation process in the field differs qualitatively – not just quantitatively – from that in the laboratory: factors which are important in the laboratory are unimportant in the field, and vice versa. This confirms our opinion (Chapter 1) that laboratory studies on their own are totally unreliable. Laboratory work should only be an adjunct to field studies. The argument that predation cannot be studied in the field is no longer valid.

(3) In the coccinellid–aphid case, the survival rate conforms to the 'random search' expression (1) at high prey densities, although the value of k varies according to aphid age-distribution and temperature. But at low prey density, the true survival rate is much higher than that predicted by 'random search' because the predators have not enough time to find all

the prey they need. For reasons argued by Frazer and Gilbert, it is preferable to think in terms of limited predator time, rather than the limited search area which many theoretical writers have invoked (cf. Hassell and May 1973). This is especially true when an animal's 'reactive distance' varies with hunger or with temperature (Holling 1965, Jones 1976*b*).

(4) In the coccinellid-aphid case, a study of the predation process alone would be inadequate, because temperature has differential effects on the predation rate and on the prey population dynamics. To understand the true relationship between predator and prey, we must necessarily study both the predation process itself and the population dynamics.

(5) Many theoreticians have defined 'population stability' as a tendency for population size to return to some equilibrium value (but see Holling 1973). That value may vary from season to season, and may never be achieved in practice, but it must exist as a theoretical entity. The coccinellid-aphid case permits no such equilibrium, even in theory. It is true that, for any given density of aphids and any given temperature, we can specify a corresponding density of ladybirds that would hold aphid numbers steady, once the aphid age-distribution had stabilized. But if the temperature increased slightly, the coccinellids would begin to drive the aphids down to extinction, and would continue to do so, even if the temperature subsequently returned to its original value. Similarly, a temporary decrease in temperature would start an increase in aphid numbers, which the ladybirds could not subsequently halt. The conventional definition of stability, *viz.* a tendency to return towards a steady state, simply does not apply because no steady state is possible, even in theory. We must add that we know of no case where such an 'equilibrium' has been demonstrated, except in the laboratory. Nor can the coccinellid-aphid case properly be regarded as an example of a 'limit cycle', or of a system which is free to vary at random within fixed limits. For the predator-prey relationship sets no upper limit to the densities of either prey or predator, and no lower limit (except zero) for the predator; while the minimum

prey density depends on both the temperature and the age-distribution of the prey.

The truth is very simple: the predators leave the alfalfa field when the prey density has sunk so low that the predators cannot find enough to eat. It might be argued that we must therefore include all the alternative food supplies available to the coccinellids elsewhere, in the study. That would be an impossible task, and it would not alter our account of the relationship between the coccinellids and the pea aphids.

(6) It would be quite impracticable to measure the effect of predation empirically, by experimental tests covering all possible combinations of predator and prey density, under all environmental conditions. Such tests could not be accurate, nor could they guarantee that all relevant factors had been considered. Therefore, the effect of some predator on its prey population, in all circumstances encountered in the field, can be predicted *only* by making a detailed field study of the predation process itself – i.e. of the behaviour of individual predators and prey – and then building the predation rate so determined into a study of the population dynamics of the prey (cf. Hagen and van den Bosch 1968). We may certainly hope that, on the basis of future experience, short-cut methods will be found, perhaps by classifying different types of predator (Chapter 8): but at present there are no short cuts, either in theory, in the laboratory or in the field.

These conclusions may be illustrated by a comparison with the work of Wratten (1973), who studied another coccinellid–aphid relationship in the laboratory, and extrapolated the results to field conditions. The following technical criticisms in no way detract from the importance of Wratten's attempt to escape from the laboratory to the field. Wratten studied larvae of the coccinellid *Adalia bipunctata* (L.), predating the lime aphid *Eucallipterus tiliae* L. on lime trees. He used Nicholson's 'area of search' argument to predict predation rates on mature trees in the field from observations of larvae searching saplings in the laboratory. We doubt if such extrapolation can be trusted: it would admittedly be difficult (but not impossible) to study search behaviour on large trees in the field. Although Wratten mentions the effect of temperature on rate of search, he has overlooked its overwhelming effect on the whole predation process, simply because that process was studied in the laboratory and not in the field. High temperatures favour the coccinellids: low temperatures favour the aphids. Wratten assumes that coccinellid larvae search continuously for sixteen hours a day. In fact they do not: our own observations on coccinellid larvae in the field show that they spend considerable periods of time doing nothing in particular. (Curiously enough, they spend some time doing 'pressups', i.e. rhythmically raising and lowering the body, for reasons unknown.) Thus Wratten very probably overestimates the true predation rate, a circumstance which merely strengthens his conclusion that the predation had little effect on aphid numbers. But this argument shows how important it is to check the estimated rate of predation by proving that, when built into a simulation of the population dynamics of the prey, it does indeed explain the observed changes in prey numbers. Without an independent check of this kind, no predation study, however realistic and detailed, can be entirely trustworthy. We shall discuss another aspect of Wratten's pioneering work in Chapter 8.

5 PLANT-HERBIVORE RELATIONSHIPS

This chapter considers two main questions. How can the mutual interactions of plant and herbivore populations be described? And do they differ significantly from other predator–prey relationships? Harper and White (1971) argue that each individual plant is itself a population of plant parts (leaves, stems etc.) with a dynamic age structure, and that plants have greater plasticity, or powers of regeneration, than animals. On this view, grasshoppers attacking plants cannot be compared with, say, ladybirds eating aphids. This chapter examines those two questions using a series of case-histories. For the same technical reasons stated in previous chapters, these cases all concern insects. Most of the case-histories concentrate attention either on the insect, or on the plant; but we shall show that it is perfectly possible to study the true interaction, which includes both the effect of the herbivore on the plant and vice versa. All these studies involve plant species with discrete growth forms, so that one plant, or plant terminal, is easily distinguished from the next. The reason is that plant density is often an important factor in itself, and must therefore be measurable.

The first case-history is that of *Masonaphis maxima* on thimbleberry (Gilbert and Gutierrez 1973). Here the aphid is extremely sensitive to the condition of its host plant, and the observed aphid fecundity gives a simple bioassay of the plant's worth to the aphid. There is an element of circularity here, since we use an aphid characteristic to assess the plant's effect on the aphid. The method tells us nothing at all about the aphid's effect on the plant, but does successfully assess the reverse effect, and the resulting plant–aphid relationship passes the 'optimum fitness' test of Chapter 3.

An equally superficial approach to the problem lies in the comparison of developmental rates of *Aphis craccivora* on different host species (Gutierrez, Havenstein *et al.* 1974). Although the aphid can complete its development on various legumes, it does so at sharply different speeds. Once again, we get useful understanding of the effect of plant on aphid, but not vice versa.

The work on cereal leaf beetle, *Oulema melanopus* (L.) (Gutierrez, Denton *et al.* 1974) comes much closer to a true insect-plant interaction. Rates of plant growth are described simply as functions of temperature and rainfall, while the insect population dynamics are represented in greater detail. Accumulated winter temperatures determine (1) over-winter survival of diapausing adult insects, (2) the timing of emergence in the spring and (3) the onset of plant growth. The density of insect larvae per plant predicts the amount of defoliation and hence the relative effect on crop yield, while the damage which the larvae inflict on the plants in turn causes the adult beetles to leave the field. Exactly what signal prompts the adults to leave is not known: but their emigration rate is observed to increase with the amount of defoliation, and is so represented in the model. Thus the reciprocal effects of plant and insect are loosely tied together, but without any intimate effect of food supply on larval development. Moreover, the simulation model does not predict absolute values for crop yields. The representation of plant growth, and its intimate effect on insect development, is therefore still incomplete.

A proper coupling of plant and herbivore must describe the basic process, *viz.* the transfer of food material from plant to animal. Such a description has been achieved for cotton. Hesketh *et al.* (1971), Baker *et al.* (1972) and McKinion *et al.* (1974) have studied the growth and development of cotton in the South-east United States. The rate of production of photosynthate, measured in terms of carbon fixation, depends on leaf mass, temperature, photoperiod and water and nitrogen supply. The photosynthate is shared out to increase the dry weight of the various parts of the plant. Uptake of dry matter through the roots is negligible, so that photosynthate production may be equated to dry weight increase, plus respiratory loss. This work describes the growth and development of a single cotton plant. Gutierrez, Falcon *et al.* (1975) used the model for photosynthate production to develop a population, or canopy, model for the growth and development of Acala cotton grown in California. Different cotton cultivars have roughly the same rates of photosynthesis (El-Sharkawy *et al.* 1965), and so the equations describing photosynthesis developed for another variety of cotton worked well for the Californian variety.

The change from a single-plant model to a population model was made in order to couple the insect populations to the plant. To predict the effect of the herbivore on the plant, and vice versa, the age-structure of both populations must be known. The population of plant parts grows by accumulation of dry matter, while the death rate is determined by plant senescence, herbivore feeding and the shedding of flowers and fruit in response to a shortage of photosynthate (cf. McKinion *et al.* 1974). The model compares daily photosynthate supply with the demands of the various parts of the plant. When the plant cannot meet all those demands, it allocates the available supply among the fruit, leaves, roots etc. according to a priority scheme. Surplus developing fruit is shed. The simulation model combines these various rules to give a remarkably accurate description of the growth of Californian cotton. Notably, it gives the correct timing of development, and explains the well-known indeterminate pattern of growth. This model steers a middle course between excessive detail on the one hand, and superficiality on the other (cf. McArthur *et al.* 1975).

Insect attack imposes an extra drain on photosynthate. Although insects require more than carbohydrate for their nutrition, phytophagous insects are generally so well adapted to their host plants that the plant supplies a proper balance of the necessary nutrients. It is therefore possible to use the insect's consumption of dry matter as an index of its total demands on the plant. This is true even in the case of aphids, which imbibe and excrete large quantities of carbohydrate (honeydew) in order to obtain sufficient amounts of other nutrients. But it is not good enough to represent insect attack simply as a photosynthate sink. The beet army worm, *Spodoptera exigua* (Hübner) and the cabbage looper, *Trichoplusia ni* (Hübner), both attack cotton leaves of a particular age-class, so causing a direct loss of leaf mass and in consequence a reduction in photosynthetic potential. It is easy to estimate the amounts consumed by these larvae, and deduct them from the stock of leaf mass in the model. The beet army worm also attacks immature fruit, which the plant consequently sheds; and as explained above, this causes a diversion of photosynthate into the production of new flowers and fruit. This effect too is easily included in the cotton model (Gutierrez, Falcon *et al.* 1975). But the insect–plant relationship is still one-sided, for although the effect of insect on plant is accurately described, the reverse effect is totally ignored. The difficulty is that these insects have several alternative hosts, so that their population dynamics do not depend on cotton alone. Stinner, Rabb and Bradley (1974) experienced a similar problem with two more cotton pests, *Heliothis zea* (Boddie) and *H. virescens* (F.) in North Carolina. Stinner *et al.* could predict the timing of *Heliothis* generations very well on the physiological time-scale, but the actual numbers were not so easily predicted.

The dual relationship has been achieved in the case of the pink boll worm, *Pectinophora gossypiella* Saunders, in the desert valleys of south eastern California (Gutierrez and Butler in prep.). Unlike the other cotton pests previously mentioned, the pink boll worm is a specific pest of cotton. It attacks both wild and cultivated cotton. Spring rains, which germinate wild cotton seed, also induce the pink boll worm to break its winter diapause. The pink boll worm has a much higher threshold for development (18°C) than does cotton (12°C) so that its development is delayed until the cotton has started to grow (Chapter 8). Attack by pink boll worm may itself cause the shedding of fruit, but the moths prefer to lay their eggs on fruit of an intermediate age which is least likely to be shed. This produces a rather complicated relationship between moth attack, photosynthate demand and fruit production, which tends to enhance the number of sites available for egglaying later in the season, and which therefore affects the subsequent population dynamics of the boll worm. The study shows how critical is the relationship between the timing of insect and plant development.

A better marriage of plant and insect has been achieved in the case of the Egyptian alfalfa weevil, *Hypera brunneipennis* (Boheman) and alfalfa (lucerne) (Gutierrez, Christensen *et al.* 1976). The alfalfa model is similar in principle to the cotton model, except that it incorporates no production of fruit or seed. Unlike cotton, alfalfa is harvested several times in one season by cutting all the stems and leaves. Regrowth therefore comes from the root reserves, and so the plants are very sensitive to heavy defoliation by the weevil, since defoliation depletes the reserves and so reduces the rate of regrowth. The model uses time-variable life-tables to represent the population dynamics of both plant and weevil. There is only one weevil generation per year. In California, the adults aestivate and migrate into the alfalfa field in autumn. The insect begins its reproductive cycle in autumn, when temperatures are falling, because it is native to areas of the Middle East which, like California, experience winter rainfall. The immigration into the alfalfa fields is triggered by temperatures *below* a threshold of 6°C, so that the proportion of adults which have emerged from aestivation is a sigmoid function of the accumulated day-degrees below that threshold. The instantaneous rate of immigration into the field is then proportional to the temperature *above* the same threshold. Thus the build-up of adults in the field at the start of the season may, in this case, be predicted from the ambient temperatures and from counts made very early in the season. Once the winter population has been started in this way, its dynamics may be described by the usual life-table approach. Adult fecundity is itself a function of accumulated temperature, because cool wet weather causes the adult moths to stop feeding, and therefore stop laying eggs.

Weevil populations commonly become large enough to defoliate the plants completely before all the larvae can mature. This causes (1) additional larval mortality, (2) a reduction in adult fecundity, both expressed as functions of the shortfall in food supply and (3) reduced accumulation of root reserves. Thus defoliation affects both the immediate growth of the weevil population and the subsequent regrowth of the plants. When these effects were estimated in the field and incorporated in the simulation model, a discrepancy appeared. The model predicted far more weevil eggs than were actually found, so revealing a failure of sampling (Chapter 7). The model correctly predicts the effects of defoliation on the weevil population and on alfalfa regrowth. Thus the alfalfa-weevil study confirms that detailed interactions between plant and herbivore may be described with photosynthate production and allocation as the key. Giese *et al.* (1975) have described similar work on alfalfa and the weevil in Indiana, but without coupling the two together.

These insect-cotton and insect-alfalfa models are essentially similar to the predator-prey models of Chapter 4. The plant must be broken down into its component parts – roots, stems, leaves and fruit – as Harper and White suggest, but there is no intrinsic difference between the plant-herbivore relationship and any other predator-prey relationship. The transfer of photosynthate from plant to herbivore takes us into the realm of energy flow, which is generally treated as an aspect of ecology quite separate from population dynamics: but the basic sub-models used for both plant and animal are, once again, the time-variable life-tables of Chapter 2.

6   ANIMAL MOVEMENT

The predator-prey and plant-herbivore relationships described so far were all studied within fairly homogeneous stands of vegetation. Directional preferences of individuals, or the distances they travelled, did not seriously disturb the overall relationship. But many predators and herbivores have to search widely for their prey or for their food plants; and almost all animals move about at some stage of their lives, to find mates or to avoid predation. Admittedly, we are not *obliged* to treat movement as a subject in its own right, since it forms part and parcel of other ecological relationships. But studies of movement require special techniques, and the species to be studied should fulfil certain requirements (Chapter 2). This chapter therefore examines animal movement, i.e. the animals' relationship to their geographical surroundings, as a separate topic.

We are indebted to Dr Broadhead for the following argument. Animal populations may be divided into four broad, but overlapping, categories.

(1) The cabbage aphid, *Brevicoryne brassicae*, offers an example of a purely sedentary population. It is true that the winged adults may move over distances of many kilometres; but the wingless aphids go through several generations on one plant, as a sedentary, self-contained unit of population. They may be studied as such: winged emigrants are treated as lost to the population.

(2) There are cases where animals move about, more or less randomly, within a fairly homogeneous environment, so that although the movement is an essential part of the population processes, it need not be studied in detail. For example, the coccinellid-aphid predation study of Chapter 4 is not a study of movement as such, although the coccinellids certainly move

about within the alfalfa field to catch their prey. The movement of any given ladybird about the field may be treated as random, even though the *speed* of movement affects the predation rate and must therefore be taken into account.

(3) There are cases where, say, a parasite reacts to a 'patchy' distribution of hosts, so that a full understanding of the parasite–host relationship must involve the geographical distributions, and not merely the overall densities, of parasite and host. A good example is the work of Broadhead and Cheke (1975) on *Mesopsocus* spp.

(4) Finally, there are the truly 'migratory' species which are unable to maintain themselves continuously in any one area, but rely for their continued existence on movement from one area to another. An excellent example is the Australian bushfly *Musca vetustissima* Walk. (Hughes and Nicholas 1974).

Obviously, these categories are not absolute. They depend on the human scale of measurement. A species which is highly motile over distances of metres may be regarded as sedentary on a scale of kilometres. The four categories also depend on the time-scale: the cabbage aphids of category (1) can be treated as sedentary only within the limits of one field season. But ecologists cannot escape their own limitations of space and time. Therefore, for purely technical reasons, we have to distinguish these four categories of population. In the first category, it is feasible to count all the aphids on one plant; but in the fourth category, it is quite impossible to count all the bushflies in Australia, and very difficult even to sample them. In the first category, it is possible to follow the fortunes of a given set of animals throughout their lifetimes; in the fourth category, individuals are elusive. There are therefore two, complementary, aspects of the technical problems posed by animal movement. The first concerns the effects of movement on the dynamics of an animal population. The second aspect, examined in Chapter 7, concerns the problems of defining, and sampling, 'populations' of animals that can move from place to place. These problems are the most severe of all those that confront the ecologist. And they are very important, for more and more cases are coming to light in which movement is an integral part of the population dynamics: not least, in those species which depend on semi-permanent breeding reservoirs, from which individuals migrate out into less favourable environments. Examples are the Western tent caterpillar *Malacasoma pluviale* (Dyar) (Wellington 1964), *Microtus* spp. (Krebs *et al.* 1969) and the Australian rabbit *Oryctolagus cuniculus* (Myers and Parker 1975).

There have been many attempts to study animal movement (Southwood 1966). The methods used include release–recapture techniques (e.g. Gilbert and Singer 1973), radio-tracking (e.g. Siniff and Jessen 1969), compilation of records of movement (Taylor *et al.* 1973) and identification of directions and rates of travel from the age-distributions and physiological condition of animals in samples taken over a wide area (Hughes and Nicholas 1974). All these methods measure net rates of movement. They estimate rates of immigration and emigration without examining the biological mechanisms involved. The estimates may be biased in favour of the most conspicuous animals, or of those that move the shortest distances. These immigration and emigration rates are purely descriptive, just as birth- and survival-rates are descriptive measures of population change (Chapter 2). To understand why the animals are moving, and to predict how the rates of movement will respond to changing circumstances, we must work at a deeper level.

The movements of ladybirds, searching for prey within an alfalfa field, belong to category (2). Therefore, to predict the predation rate, we need not study those movements in detail – which is fortunate, since we cannot track the flight of adult beetles over distances of more than a few metres. But movements of adult beetles into, and out of, the field in response to changes in aphid numbers are crucially important to the population dynamics of both aphids and coccinellids. Such movements belong to category (3). Dr P. M. Ives (unpublished) has used both release–recapture methods and traps to estimate movement of ladybird beetles from plot to plot in the field. The rates of movement may then be correlated with weather conditions and with aphid density. In certain circumstances, coccinellids arrive in large numbers and drive the aphid density down to levels far below those required for successful coccinellid reproduction. But beetle movement, voracity and fecundity are geared together in a way that renders the coccinellids incapable of exterminating their prey – except very locally, within a few square metres at most. Indeed, successful coccinellid breeding does not begin until the aphid density is so high that the coccinellids cannot prevent a further increase in aphid numbers. Very reasonably, the ladybirds leave the alfalfa field when the aphid density sinks so low that they cannot catch enough aphids to maintain their own body weight: but they may also leave the field after they have laid eggs there, even though the aphid density remains high. Why they do so is not understood, but the result is that the coccinellid larvae, which hatch from the eggs, do not have to compete with their parents for prey. Ives' work therefore gives a good account of the effect of movements in category (3) on the population dynamics, within the field, of both predator and prey.

Broadhead and Cheke (1975) adopt another approach to movements in category (3). They show how the local distributions of parasites and hosts interact to affect the rate of parasitization. They have not investigated the patterns of movement that give rise to those distributions, nor have they examined the other biological mechanisms that determine the population dynamics of host and parasite. In particular, we do not know whether the parasites respond solely to the distribution of their hosts, or to other stimuli as well. This work is therefore essentially descriptive, i.e. it cannot predict how the parasite–host relationship would react to new circumstances: but it does give good understanding of the events observed in the field. This approach is therefore very productive, provided that we recognize that we cannot deduce, from an observed distribution, the biological mechanisms that gave rise to that distribution. For example, a negative binomial distribution of numbers of animals may be generated in several sharply different ways (Southwood 1966). Similarly, any geographical distribution of animals may be generated by a variety of movement patterns, which would produce very diverse outcomes in other circumstances. For predictive purposes, therefore, it is essential to study the movement process itself, and to link the *individual's* behaviour to the subsequent effect on the *population* (Chapter 4).

With these considerations in mind, Jones (1976b,c) has studied the cabbage white butterfly, *Pieris rapae* L. That species was chosen solely because it satisfies all, or very nearly all, the desiderata for studies of movement and of population dynamics (Chapter 2). The object is to predict the consequences, for the population, of the movements of individual animals in a variety of natural circumstances. For details of the following argument, see Chapter 11. Jones has developed fairly comprehensive behavioural descriptions of the movements of both butterflies and caterpillars; incorporated those descriptions into simulation models of the movement processes; and used the models to predict rates of migration from area to area, and the numbers of host plants which are discovered within each area, in any specified circumstances. These migration and encounter rates may then be fed into a 'variable life-table', which specifies the subsequent population dynamics.

In this case, the translation from the level of individual behaviour to the level of population dynamics presents no difficulty at all. The rules of movement of adult females – degree of directionality, preferred directions, attraction to host plants, probabilities of landing and egglaying, and the effects of the butterflies' own physiological condition – were deduced from field observations. Those rules, built into a stochastic simulation model, successfully describe the movements of individual butterflies, and consequently the pattern of egglaying, over a wide range of circumstances. Dr P. M. Ives (unpublished) has shown that the butterflies do not discriminate between plants according to the presence or absence of caterpillars, or of previously-laid eggs. Nor do they behave differently at different adult densities. So the simulation model need not consider the current population dynamics of either adults or caterpillars. The model is technically a 'directed random walk' (Chapter 11), with complex rules of movement to decide the direction of each successive step.

The distribution and numbers of eggs laid affect the survival of the caterpillars which hatch from those eggs. If too many eggs are laid on one plant, the caterpillars will eat out the plant and then starve. The danger is mitigated by the caterpillars' ability to find new plants. Jones (1976a) therefore studied the movements of caterpillars too, and made a stochastic simulation of their movement which can predict survival rates for any combination of plant sizes, distribution and density. The movement pattern of *P. rapae* caterpillars differs sharply from that of two other Lepidopterous species which attack the same host plants, but caterpillar behaviour is in each case well adapted to the normal circumstances of the species concerned.

The movement models for both butterflies and caterpillars have been tested experimentally. In one experiment, numerous caterpillars were placed on the central plants of a field plot of small cabbage plants. The caterpillars were expected to defoliate their original plants and search for new ones; the pattern of redistribution could then be compared with that predicted by the simulation model of their search behaviour. But the experiment failed because the caterpillars were all destroyed by predatory yellow-jacket wasps (Vespidae). The tests of the model of adult movement were more successful. The distributions of eggs laid in field plots containing different sizes, species and arrangements of plants were compared with the model's predictions. For example, the model predicted that plant spacing should influence the number of eggs laid in a plot. When plots of cabbages were planted with different plant spacings, the numbers of eggs laid agreed very well with those predicted.

Animal movement

By building the predicted survival rates of caterpillars into a (deterministic) population model, it is possible to examine the effect of the butterflies' egglaying behaviour on the subsequent dynamics of the population. If a butterfly does not move at all, but lays all her eggs on one plant, the resultant caterpillars are likely to starve. But if she lays only one egg on each plant encountered, she is unlikely to find enough plants on which to lay all her eggs. Her rules of movement and egglaying must therefore strike a balance, to maximize population 'fitness' (Chapter 3). Although *P. rapae* has entered both Canada and Australia from Europe within the last hundred years, it behaves in sharply different ways in the two countries, in agreement with the different local conditions. It is therefore possible to gauge the effect of the movement process itself on the population dynamics.

Jones' methods have a further advantage. They allow us to determine, from the animals' point of view (not the human point of view), the degree of 'patchiness' of the environment. A stand of plants consists of individual plants arranged in some sort of pattern. For convenience, the ecologist usually divides the stand into a series of patches; within each patch, the distribution of plants is treated as purely random. But what is the right size of patch? We might (at one extreme) treat all the plants in an area of several kilometres as a single patch, or we might (at the other extreme) regard each individual plant as a patch. Clearly, the elephant's idea of a uniform patch will differ from the ant's. So the appropriate size of patch depends on the animal's pattern of movement. Jones' model of butterfly movement tells us how close a butterfly must come to a patch of plants before its flight pattern is significantly affected by the presence of the plants. That distance defines the appropriate size of each patch: two clumps of plants separated by a lesser distance are, from a butterfly's point of view, a single patch. The distance varies according to the number of eggs which the butterfly has still to lay. This circumstance is no artefact of the model, but a biological reality.

An obvious objection is that Jones' methods can describe

only the short-distance movements of *P. rapae*. We cannot track an adult butterfly throughout her lifetime. The objection is partly overcome by rearing butterflies to lay coloured eggs (Parker and Pinnell 1972) and showing that the distribution of their eggs, over longer distances, agrees with that predicted by extrapolation of the short-distance movement patterns (Jones and Gossard, in prep.). But it is quite true that Jones' methods remain firmly within category (3). There are no really satis-factory methods of studying animal movements in category (4) over distances of many kilometres. With radio tracking, it is very difficult to individually mark a large enough sample of animals. Other methods, except perhaps radar tracking, fail to satisfy the requirement of Chapter 2 that *all* the animals – not just some conspicuous fraction of the whole population – shall be observable. The problems of measuring long-distance movements are unsolved, and we offer no solution to them here.

7 EXPERIMENTS AND SAMPLES

All the methods used in previous chapters depend on the collection of reliable data. Suppose that we wish to estimate the number of grasshoppers in a field, and that – unknown to us – the true number is ten thousand. It would be quite impracticable to count them all, and so we take samples to estimate the density. Evidently, a sample which includes one-hundredth of the area of the field should, on average, contain a hundred grasshoppers. But particular methods of sampling may return answers which are, *on average*, less than a hundred, perhaps because they concentrate on sparsely-populated parts of the field, or because they disturb the grasshoppers. Such methods are said to be 'negatively biased'. Alternatively, particular methods of sampling may return answers which are, *on average*, greater than one hundred. Such methods are 'positively biased'. An unbiased sampling method gives an *average* count of one hundred: but it is 'inaccurate' if the individual sample counts often vary greatly from the true value of one hundred. Every individual sample count will be close to the true value of one hundred, and therefore reliable, only if the sampling method is both unbiased and accurate. By far the most serious problem in ecology today is not any difficulty of theory, analysis or interpretation: it is the difficulty of finding, and implementing, accurate and unbiased sampling methods in the field. At the same time, ecologists are beginning to make experiments in the field, either to collect data or to test hypotheses and models; this chapter will examine such sampling and experimental techniques. As in previous chapters, we shall have to rely on our own limited experience, so that our conclusions must be tentative.

Samples
Southwood (1966) surveys the problems of sampling animals in

the field, and his excellent book is essential reading. But it must be added that the variable life-tables introduced in Chapter 2 (and elaborated in Chapter 9) largely supersede Southwood's fixed life-tables, as well as the related methods of analysis such as key-factor analysis (Varley *et al.* 1973). That is because variable life-tables offer far greater realism, and biological insight, than the old methods. But the sampling methods must be correspondingly more rigorous. Here we shall state some general principles – which only reinforce what Southwood has to say – and illustrate them with particular case-histories.

The sample must represent the defined 'population' of animals or plants which we wish to investigate. It is not always easy to define what we mean by a plant or animal population, but for practical purposes we usually take it to mean 'all the individuals in some defined geographical area'. If this definition is to make ecological sense, the area in question must be sufficiently large that most individuals remain within it throughout the period of study, or during their lifetimes. It is no use choosing an area so small that the individual animals constantly wander in and out of it. The area may therefore be measured in square metres for aphids, but in square kilometres for elephants. It may be a single plant for caterpillars, and a whole continent for the butterflies which develop from those caterpillars. In other words, the rates of immigration and emigration from the area must be reasonably small over the time-period of the study; in fact, those rates actually specify what ecologists mean by a 'population'. Unfortunately, immigration and emigration rates are usually unknown at the start of the investigation, so that suitable study areas – and therefore study populations – must be guessed from preliminary knowledge of the species' biology. Different areas will be appropriate to different species, even within one study: rabbits may be studied in one square kilometre, whereas the eagles which prey on those rabbits may require hundreds of square kilometres. The 'area' which defines the population need not be strictly geographical at all. The population might be defined as 'all the aphids on a particular tree'. But, very often, an animal population is empirically defined to be all the individuals in a particular area which is covered by the particular kind of vegetation suited to those animals, and which is surrounded by a different type of habitat, expected to restrict immigration and emigration. Our task is then to take accurate, unbiased samples from that population.

Having defined the population, we must next choose the sampling unit, which might be a plant leaf, a whole plant or an area of ground. A sample will then comprise all the animals found on a specified number of such units. The choice of unit is dictated partly by convenience, but mainly by the requirement that the sample shall be unbiased, or 'representative'. Southwood (*op. cit.*) lists six important criteria, originally laid down by Morris (1955), for the choice of sampling units.

The only way to get an *unbiased* sample is, by definition, to ensure that every animal in the population has the same chance of appearing in the sample. (If the population is heterogeneous in some identifiable way, it may pay to 'stratify' the sampling, in which case, different sections of the population are sampled separately. But this does not affect the main principle.) We should therefore choose a sampling method to which all the animals are equally accessible; and in particular, each animal must be given no chance to decide for itself whether or not it shall appear in the sample. This requirement at once rules out most – but not quite all – trapping methods, since it is well established (Southwood 1966) that different individuals respond differentially to traps. It is no defence to say that we will define our population to include only those animals liable to trapping, because the probability of trapping a given individual varies greatly according to its hunger, sexual status, the local temperature, the type of trap and many other factors.

The population at risk thus varies from day to day, for purely technical reasons. It may therefore be very difficult – if not impossible, with present technology – to find an unbiased sampling method for some given species of animal, and this is an important consideration when choosing suitable species for ecological work (Chapter 2). It may be permissible to use a sampling method which is known to be biased, if we can be confident that the extent of the bias is known under all the sampling conditions encountered. To estimate the bias, the method must be calibrated against some unbiased sampling method, possibly too expensive for regular use. Once an unbiased (or nearly so) method has been found, accuracy becomes a matter of sample size: the bigger the sample, the more accurate the answer. Southwood recommends aiming for a standard error equal to 10% of the mean, and that is indeed a desirable level of accuracy in ecological work, although it is not always achieved in practice (Chapter 9). The rules giving the sample size required for any specified accuracy appear in many statistical texts: unfortunately they are misprinted in Southwood's first edition. It is obviously undesirable if, to achieve the desired accuracy, we have to remove a large fraction of the population. This is one reason why there are so few studies of animal populations at very low density. Another reason is that, at low densities, the animals often cannot be found at all.

We shall illustrate these simple, but all-important, principles by two case-histories: insects on alfalfa (lucerne) and on cotton. For many species of insect – including aphids – which infest small plants, the plant itself is the most convenient sampling unit, because the individuals on one plant form a coherent sub-population. Although some individuals certainly move from plant to plant, in general each juvenile aphid remains on one plant during its whole development, so that density-dependent competition for food or living space affects all the aphids on each individual plant, largely irrespective of events on other plants. Thus the plant forms a natural population unit, and is therefore a convenient sampling unit too. Larger kinds of plant may be too big to use as sampling units (Maelzer 1976). In the case of alfalfa, each plant initially forms a single stem, or 'terminal', but as it grows it produces numerous side-terminals, each bearing its own group of aphids. We might therefore sample the insects, using either one plant or one 'terminal' as the sampling unit. In the case of young plants, those two units coincide: but in the case of older plants, the whole plant is inconveniently large, while the 'terminals' are ill-defined. Purely to avoid the problems of sampling old plants, Frazer and Gilbert deliberately cut their alfalfa more often than normal commercial practice dictates.

Strictly speaking, the plants to be sampled should be selected at random, using tables of random numbers to mark down each chosen plant. In practice, strictly random sampling takes far too much time, and instead we choose sample plants by walking down a length of row without looking at it, stopping at an arbitrary point, and taking the first plant that comes to hand. This method is likely to give biased results, partly because some plants are more conspicuous than others; partly because humans tend to avoid extreme examples and instead choose 'representative' plants; and partly because, as Southwood notes, marginal areas tend to be under-sampled. However objective we try to be, bias creeps in unless the sampling is strictly random. We shall return to this question of bias shortly.

The sample size may be roughly determined as follows. If the aphids are distributed at random between plants according to a Poisson distribution, a count of N aphids will have a standard error of $\sqrt{N}$. Therefore, to achieve the desired 10% standard error, N must be at least 100, and so we aim to sample enough plants to give at least 100 aphids in the whole sample. At the same time, we require a minimum of (say) 50 plants, to ensure that the whole crop area is adequately covered. This sample size must be increased (a) when, as usually happens at high population densities, the insects show a contagious distribution, i.e. are excessively numerous on some plants and rare on others, or (b) if an accurate estimate of the numbers of individuals of each instar (not just total numbers) is required. The same kind of consideration governs the numbers of animals used in laboratory trials to determine temperature thresholds, rates of development and fecundity, etc. (Campbell et al. 1974).

Since the coccinellid predators of aphids move rapidly from plant to plant, Frazer and Gilbert sampled them per unit length of row, rather than per plant. This they did by carefully searching 30 cm lengths of row for all the ladybirds, moving and stationary, conspicuous and hidden. Conventional methods using sweep-nets or suction machines are unreliable for quantitative work: at best they indicate the presence or absence of large numbers of beetles. (Hughes (1955), quoted by Southwood (1966), has shown how dependent sweep-net samples are on the prevailing conditions.) These coccinellid row-counts are best done at high temperatures, when the beetles are active and therefore easily seen. By contrast, aphid samples are best taken in the cool conditions of early morning, since at warm temperatures, aphids of many species readily fall off their host plants at the slightest disturbance.

Whenever different units are used to sample different life-stages or species – as is very often unavoidable – the two kinds of units must be reconciled, so that the numerical estimates can be put on the same footing. In the present case, aphids were sampled per plant, and coccinellids per 30 cm of row. The necessary conversion factor is clearly the number of plants in 30 cm of row, and the obvious remedy is to count the number of plants in selected lengths of row. This number, incidentally, changes every time the plants are cut. But here we encounter a difficulty. Aphids are much less common on the short under-storey plants, which are inaccessible to sampling, than on the larger plants that form the canopy. The actual number of insects in 30 cm of row is consistently about half that predicted when we multiply the average density of aphids per plant observed in the samples by the counted number of plants in the length of row. The regular aphid samples must therefore be *calibrated* from time to time, by enclosing whole lengths of plant row in plastic bags, cutting the plants and counting the total numbers of aphids per bag. This calibration also corrects for any possible bias caused by the fact that the samples are not taken strictly randomly.

It is much more difficult to calibrate the counts of

coccinellids. When known numbers of beetles were released into field cages containing alfalfa, only about 25% could be counted at any one time: the other ladybirds were well hidden in the stubble. Dr P. M. Ives (unpublished) has successfully tested and used the capture-recapture method on adult coccinellids. That method is time-consuming, and its accuracy is inevitably low, but it may be used to calibrate counts made in the open field at various temperatures. The most direct method of sampling ladybirds is both time-consuming and destructive. It involves cutting the plants in a length of row down to the roots and then removing the loose soil and debris with a powerful vacuum device. Since it is unusual to find more than half a dozen coccinellids per metre length of row, this method requires the destruction of considerable amounts of alfalfa if it is to give satisfactory accuracy. The significant point here is that the most difficult part of a predator–prey study in the field has proved to be not the estimation of predation rates as they vary with predator, prey densities and other factors, but simply the technical problem of estimating the predator density. If the sampling problems cannot be overcome, they rule out the particular species concerned as candidates for this kind of work.

Gutierrez, Christensen *et al.* (1976) encountered similar problems when studying the Egyptian alfalfa weevil, *Hypera brunneipennis*. The counts of larvae greatly exceeded the counts of the eggs from which those larvae had hatched (Chapter 5). Since the possibility of immigration could be discounted, this revealed a sampling failure. Previous workers had thought that weevil eggs are laid on the plant itself, but investigation showed that most eggs are in fact laid on plant debris in the undergrowth. Ignorance of the true biology therefore rendered a large proportion of the eggs immune to sampling.

The sampling of insects on cotton raises further considerations. They arise partly because cotton plants are large, discrete and easily distinguished; and partly because different species of insect are found on different parts of the plant – on leaves, flowers or bolls. Such sampling problems are characteristic of large plants and trees. Since plant density is an important factor affecting the rate of cotton growth, Gutierrez, Falcon *et al.* (1975) used a simulation model which predicts the growth, not of single plants, but of all the plants on a fixed area of land. The model describes the growth of the various parts (roots, leaves etc.) of the plants. Insect population densities were likewise sampled, not on a per-plant basis, but per unit area of land, irrespective of plant density. To determine which parts of the plant were attacked by each species of insect, entire plants were included in the samples. Thus the sampling entailed the destruction of all the plants in a sample area – which was feasible only because the study was made on a stand of cotton covering several hundred hectares.

Field experiments

The principles of experimentation in field ecology are the same as in any other science; but field experiments have been rare in ecology, possibly because they are exceptionally difficult to perform. Many ecological experiments have been done in the laboratory, but they can only be an adjunct to work in the field (Chapter 4). Any kind of experiment involves the comparison of events when some treatment is applied with events when that treatment is not applied (control). In biology, it is usually too risky to apply treatment and control in sequence to the same material, partly because other relevant circumstances may change at the same time and partly because of the danger of residual treatment effects. Field experimentation therefore demands a set of comparable but independent plots, to some of which the treatments may be applied, while others serve as controls.

R. A. Fisher developed the classical theory of experimental design for just this purpose, and his designs – randomized blocks, Latin squares etc. – are, of course, universal in agricultural field trials for accurately assessing the rather small (but economically important) differences between

Experiments and samples

crop varieties or fertilizer treatments. But in ecology, we can rarely afford the luxury of extensive replication and concomitant randomization, because we cannot afford to set up, and monitor, large numbers of comparable, independent populations. The amount of work required to follow the course of a single population in any detail is very considerable; to follow a dozen populations at once, except very superficially, is usually impossible. Therefore, only a few field plots can be maintained at any one time. Moreover, it is usually impossible to choose, in advance, a size of plot that will guarantee independence of the ecological events on different plots. This is the same problem as that of defining a population, mentioned above: we need to know in advance how far the animals concerned can move during the course of the experiment, so that we can use plots large enough (or far enough apart) to rule out significant interference from one plot. to the next. We must choose plots large enough for independence, but close enough for comparability. Without previous knowledge of rates of movement of all the animals concerned, we cannot do so with any confidence. The well-known replacement experiments of Watson and Jenkins (1968), imitated by several subsequent workers, depend on the knowledge that the birds will not move out of their breeding territories during the course of the experiment. When studying *Masonaphis maxima*, Gilbert and Gutierrez (1973) were able to measure the relationship between density and fecundity experimentally in the field, solely because the aphid has discrete generations, and moves from plant to plant only at the end of each generation. Parker and Pinnell (1972) used an ingenious method of marking to detect movements of *Pieris rapae* from plot to plot. In most cases, there is no such easy assurance of independence.

But ecologists are concerned only with rather large and obvious differences. The 10% differences so important to agronomists are trivial to ecologists. We may therefore follow the example of the biochemists, who generally concern themselves with differences of 100% or more, and who rarely indulge in extensive replication within any one experiment. The analogy with biochemistry is not complete for the following reason. Biochemists, working in well-controlled conditions, have good experience of the amount of natural, or 'background', variation which they are likely to encounter. When biochemists assert, without reference to standard errors, that such-and-such a treatment difference is meaningful, they mean that the difference is far larger than could be expected from natural variation in the absence of the treatment. Ecologists have, at present, scant experience of the amount of natural variation to be expected in field experiments, nor can they easily control it. Thus the ecologist has the worst of both worlds – he cannot rely on previous experience, as the biochemist does, nor can he afford the large numbers of replicates used in agricultural field trials to estimate the residual variation within each trial. The obvious answer, at first sight, is to impose very drastic treatments which produce 'all-or-none' effects. But if some treatment completely eliminates some particular category of animal, a treatment twice as severe can have no greater effect. Therefore, if we wish to *estimate* the effect of some treatment (and compare it with our predictions), that effect must be large and obvious, but not 'all-or-none'; and we still need some assurance, however imprecise, that the observed effect was indeed due to the imposed treatment, rather than to natural 'background' variation.

We shall now discuss some attempts to put these notions into practice. Gilbert and Hughes (1971) tried to test their understanding of the relationship between *Brevicoryne brassicae* and its parasite *Diaeretiella rapae* in a replicated experiment using twelve miniature plots of kale. Parasitized aphids were added to six of the plots, while the other six received only unparasitized aphids. To avoid contamination by adult aphids and parasites arriving from outside, the experiment was done in a remote open valley surrounded by pine forests. As a result, the plants were in a region where crucifers were scarce. Large numbers of cabbage white

Experiments and samples

butterflies (*Pieris rapae* L.) arrived and laid eggs on the plants, which in consequence were heavily damaged, even though hundreds of caterpillars were removed by hand. Thus the idea of doing the experiment in an isolated region, in order to minimize outside interference, was rewarded by the unforeseen, concentrated attack of a very mobile pest. It is doubtful whether the isolation would have been effective anyway, since subsequent knowledge of parasite behaviour suggests that the adult parasites would have spread rapidly to all the plots, which were only 50 m apart. This underlines the difficulty of ensuring the independence of the different plots. But by far the greatest difficulty in this experiment was to get it started at all. Leaf disks bearing adult aphids (parasitized or otherwise) were pinned to the uninfested plants, in the expectation that the aphids would establish themselves on the plants. In this way, the experiment would begin with known numbers of aphids of known age. But many of these aphids failed to establish themselves, and it was impossible to count those that did, or to determine whether they were parasitized or not. This ruined the experiment at the start: for if the initial numbers and age-distributions are unknown, we cannot predict the subsequent course of events for comparison with that actually observed. This acute difficulty, of starting an experiment by releasing known numbers of animals, will be even greater in the case of vertebrates which ˙establish individual territories and hierarchies.

Frazer and Gilbert (1976) therefore tried a different tack. They used field cages to compare the progress of pea aphid populations on alfalfa, in the presence and absence of coccinellid predators. The cages served to keep known numbers of ladybirds in, and incidentally to keep some other predators (syrphids and chrysopids) out. Instead of artificially introducing known numbers of aphids, Frazer and Gilbert allowed the aphid population to establish itself, and then took samples to estimate the initial density and age-distribution. This approach proved to be more successful, but it requires that the cages shall be large enough, and the aphids numerous enough, to permit accurate initial samples which still leave most of the plants in each cage intact.

A good estimate of the age-distribution requires a larger sample than a good estimate of total numbers: and the initial age-distribution must be known for the following reason. A mature population, consisting mostly of adults, will begin to increase sooner than a young population composed of juveniles, who must wait to mature before they begin to reproduce. Therefore, differences in rates of increase, ostensibly due to predation, may in fact be due to differences in the initial age-distribution. Admittedly, the initial age-distribution influences the population dynamics during the first two or three generations only; but in this case, each experiment could run for only a limited period of time before the alfalfa plants grew too large to permit accurate sampling of the aphid population. Fortunately, this time-period was long enough to reveal those consistent effects of predation which the experiments were designed to test. But the problem of estimating the initial aphid density and age-distribution was accentuated by a further circumstance. The effect of ladybird predation decreases sharply as the temperature declines. So a period of cool temperatures at the start of the experiment would permit the aphids to increase to a point where the coccinellids, unless quite unrealistically numerous, could have no measurable effect on aphid numbers. Moreover, we were concerned to examine the effect of predation at low aphid densities, rather than at high densities where predation becomes effectively a random process. Therefore, each experiment was begun at low aphid density, which only increases the difficulty of obtaining accurate initial samples.

It may be objected that the use of field cages makes the results of an experiment almost as unrealistic as if it were done in artificial laboratory conditions. In fact, conditions in the cages were closely similar to those in the open field. The cages were designed to admit sunlight, fresh air, and rain. The day-time temperatures recorded in the cages were only one or two degrees higher than outside: night-time temperatures were no

Experiments and samples

different. Later work by Frazer, Gilbert, Ives and Raworth, which used field cages as controls (no predation) to study predation rates in the open field, has confirmed that, so far as the coccinellid–aphid relationship is concerned, conditions inside the cages were well within the normal range experienced in the open field.

But these cage experiments raise a problem of interpretation that is likely to plague many ecological experiments in the field. It concerns the possibility of serious interaction with other factors. Using laboratory estimates of aphid fecundity, we could reproduce the observed rate of aphid increase, when no ladybirds were present, only by invoking a 70% 'background' mortality: and the age-distributions showed that this mortality must be imposed almost entirely on the newly-born first-instar aphids. The cause of the mortality is unknown, but it probably represents both a reduction in fecundity and predation by harvest-men and spiders. This 70% level of mortality is quite usual in the field, and without it the experiment must have failed, since the aphid density would otherwise have increased far too fast, leaving the coccinellids no time to demonstrate their powers of predation. But the whole object of cage experiments is to obtain a clear-cut difference between treatment and control, with reasonable assurance that ecological events in the different cages are independent, so that the difference may be used to measure the effect of the treatment. Where there is heavy background mortality of unknown origin, it is difficult to exclude the possibility that the effect of the treatment – in this case, ladybird predation – is not simply superimposed on the background mortality, but interacts strongly with it. This would render the experiment uninterpretable. Fortunately, in the coccinellid case, the possibility of serious interaction can be excluded; for individual ladybirds are observed to hunt independently of other predators. Even so, the predation relationship is still sufficiently complex that any one of these cage experiments would be unconvincing on its own; but three different experiments, covering a wide range of conditions, gave

68

consistent and satisfactory results. Thus the coccinellid-aphid experiments, although far from perfect, were adequate for their purpose.

Jones (1976c) has used field experiments to test predictions derived from studies of behaviour (Chapter 6). As in the case of *Brevicoryne brassicae*, one experiment failed because of the unforeseen intervention of another species, *viz.* a predatory Vespid wasp which destroyed the experimental populations. Ironically enough, Jones was studying the very species, *Pieris rapae*, which had ruined the previous experiment on *B. brassicae*! But Jones' other experiments, designed to test the predicted reactions of butterflies to different types and distributions of plants, were successful. It is easier to test plant-herbivore models than predator-prey models, simply because plants may be manipulated more easily than animals in the open field.

These experiments (and others not mentioned here) have made one thing very clear. An ecological experiment, like an ecological analysis (Chapter 1), is essentially dynamic. When something unexpected begins to happen during the course of an experiment, we must decide whether or not to intervene in response. If we intervene, we shall not know what would have happened if we had not intervened, and vice versa. It is therefore very desirable to design the experiment with as much replication as possible, so that if intervention becomes necessary, we can intervene on some plots and not on others. But, as previously mentioned, the total number of plots is severely limited; so the initial design should be very, very simple.

8 WHAT USE IS IT?

We have now shown, at least to our own satisfaction, that the technical problems can be solved. It is perfectly possible to study the various parts of an ecological relationship in the field, and to build them into realistic 'variable life-tables' which specify the ever-changing birth and survival rates (and where necessary, the immigration and emigration rates too) of the plant and animal populations concerned. But mere methodology is useless, unless it offers us ecological understanding or practical utility. So what has this particular approach to offer?

Our first emotion is surprise that it should be possible at all: that ecological relationships, even those specially chosen for their tractability, should be capable of detailed analysis. Anyone who casually observes the flight of a butterfly from plant to plant might well despair of describing it quantitatively, yet Jones (1976b) has shown that it depends on only seven basic parameters, which admittedly vary according to the internal and external conditions experienced by the butterfly. The methodology therefore offers a very comforting assurance that ecological research is not impossible – that ecological relationships in the field are not so hopelessly complex that they defy analysis. This point is far from trivial. Perhaps the greatest advantage of the method, therefore, is that it obliges us to study *all* the relevant parts of a relationship and to get quantitative agreement between observation and prediction. Too often in the past, ecologists have studied particular aspects of some ecological situation, yet have completely overlooked other, equally important aspects. Therefore, we cannot over-emphasize this simple argument: that changes in population numbers can be understood only if we can identify all the important biological factors which determine the birth- and survival-rates and can estimate their quantitative effects. Those birth- and survival-rates in turn are most easily understood when we use the most appropriate time-scale, which is not necessarily calendar time. The worked examples in Part 2 illustrate this simple argument in detail. In this chapter, we shall first survey some very general technical points and then consider whether the results are worth while.

Technical considerations

In a very narrow sense, we can claim that the main problems are already solved, since the object of ecological research has been identified (Chapter 3) and the worked examples have shown that the various types of ecological relationship can be studied satisfactorily. It is true that we have not discussed certain types of ecological relationship – notably competition – at all. But if animals compete, they compete for something – food, space or mates – and the competition is part and parcel of the process of finding that something. (Within-species competition is an integral part of many of the ecological relationships mentioned in this book.) Therefore, until we discover the existence of general principles governing all types of competition, we need not treat competition as a category of ecological relationship in its own right. There are certainly some rather specialized types of relationship, e.g. that between flowering plants and their pollinators, which have not been mentioned; but they can evidently be tackled in the same general way (cf. Gilbert 1975).

There are, however, plenty of technical problems still to be overcome. The main difficulty is that, at present, we are obliged to choose those species which are most tractable (Chapter 1). It is no bad thing to say so explicitly, since research administrators, who generally lack personal experience of intensive field work, insist only too often that some economically important, but very intractable animal must be studied. Two notable examples are the Canadian spruce budworm, *Choristoneura fumiferana* (Clem.) (Morris 1963), which occurs, usually at very low densities, thirty metres up a tree; and the Australian bushfly, *Musca vetustissima* Walk., whose individuals may be blown across half a continent (Hughes and Nicholas 1974). At the same time, the choice of suitable species is steadily widening. Some of the species mentioned in this book, e.g. the cereal leaf beetle and the various pests of cotton, were originally chosen for their economic importance, not because they satisfied the desiderata of Chapter 1; yet they have proved to be tractable. We have, indeed, been surprised to find how tractable they are. Conversely, the pea aphid living on alfalfa certainly was chosen for its suitability, yet the sampling problems were later found to be fairly acute.

Very recently, the voluminous data on the rabbit, *Oryctolagus cuniculus* (L.), collected over the past twenty years by the CSIRO rabbit group (Myers 1971), have been analysed in terms of 'variable life-tables'. As a mammalian pest, the rabbit is second only to man: and for that reason, it has been very intensively studied at considerable expense. So far as we know, the appropriate data have been collected for no other wild mammal. This rabbit work has shown that it is very difficult to get accurate estimates of survival rates, as they vary with time, from samples of mammals collected from time to time in the field – although it certainly is possible to estimate *average* survival rates in this way (Caughley 1966, Sinclair 1974). To give a good estimate of the age-distribution, each sample should contain at least 100 to 200 individuals and the regular loss of such numbers of animals will, in many cases, seriously affect the local population dynamics. Moreover, most current techniques for determining individual ages of mammals are inaccurate. By contrast, many insect species occur in large numbers and their different age-groups (instars) are readily distinguished. The only satisfactory estimates of rabbit survival rates were obtained by laboriously following cohorts of marked animals, in the field, from the cradle to the grave. This work therefore shows how important it is to choose animals that can be *seen* in the field (Chapter 2). On the other hand, the rabbit samples give much better estimates of

72

reproductive rates than can be obtained for insects. Each sample gives the proportion of pregnant females and the number of embryos in each litter – whereas insect reproductive rates, which are very sensitive to changes in the parent's food supply, are far harder to estimate in the field.

Thus the examples in this book are restricted to insects, purely by reason of cost and sampling difficulties, both of which curtail practical ecological work of whatever kind. At present, we do not know whether the range of species to which these techniques can be applied, is narrow or broad. If they can be applied only to a limited range of species, any ecological principles deduced from the results may apply only to a subset of all species. That consideration, although important, does not greatly deter us at present, when valid ecological principles of any kind are in painfully short supply.

It is clearly not every ecological question which is susceptible to this approach. Yet it does satisfactorily overcome the problem of realism versus generality. That problem has been stated by Holling (1966), and need not be repeated here. The studies mentioned earlier are fairly realistic, accurate and complete; and as we shall argue later, a series of such studies can furnish the comparisons from which generalizations (if they exist at all) may be deduced. This approach therefore offers a half-way house between sweeping superficiality on the one hand, and trivial detail on the other. But we must add to Holling's four desiderata – realism, precision, completeness, and generality – a fifth, namely practical utility. The reason is that, in a complex subject like ecology, our task is not merely to elucidate biological events, but to find the best overall way of looking at the subject. The question is not merely 'Which comes first, the chicken or the egg?', but rather 'Which point of view is preferable – the chicken's, or the egg's, or some other?' The theory of Chapter 3 offers one answer, but another must be the empirical one – what point of view best tells us how to manipulate ecological events in the field? Later in the chapter, therefore, we shall consider the practical possibilities of this approach.

What use is it?

Some positive technical conclusions arise from the studies already made.

(1) It is indeed possible to treat individual ecological relationships as isolated case histories. The relationships within a complete ecosystem are not linked together so tightly that they cannot be disentangled. But the larger task of putting these relationships together to make a complete ecosystem has yet to be attempted.

(2) The work on predation and on movement makes it clear that we must often work at the level of individual behaviour, and connect it to the consequences for the population as a whole. Indeed, behaviour actually defines the species for the ecologist: for if two different kinds of animal always behaved in the same way, we should treat them as varieties of a single species.

(3) The methods needed to analyse the varied types of relationship so far studied have all proved rather similar. This is not very surprising, since most of those relationships involve the transfer of biomass from one organism to another: but the individual components involved in each relationship are quite similar in style. The 'variable life-table' describes the growth of plant and animal populations equally well, and the component mechanisms—plants setting seed, or animals giving birth—can be described in precisely similar terms. We do not think that this is an artefact, nor is it an automatic consequence of the emphasis on population dynamics.

(4) In the cases studied so far, there have been few interactions involving more than two species at once, doubtless because the chances are slim that individuals of more than two species should meet at once. There are several exceptions. One is the observation that an aphid in the later stages of parasitization becomes less liable to coccinellid predation than an unparasitized aphid (Frazer and Gilbert 1976). Since the parasite kills the aphid very soon afterwards, and pupates inside the corpse, this is scarcely a three-species interaction at all, but mainly a two-species interaction between coccinellid

and parasite. It is treated as such in the simulation model. The selective predation of parasitized walnut aphids, *Chromaphis juglandicola* (Kaltenbach), by Argentine ants, *Iridomyrmex humilis* (Mayr) (Frazer and van den Bosch 1973) may be treated in the same way. Three-species interactions certainly do occur when disease makes animals more vulnerable to predation – as rabbits suffering from myxomatosis become more vulnerable to fox and cat predation. But so far as we know, three-species interactions are unimportant at the behavioural level, however common they may be at the statistical level of population numbers. If this is so, an ecosystem need be no more than an assemblage of two-species interactions at the behavioural level: and to study a complete ecosystem, we need do no more than investigate the two-species relationships, as described in this book, and then consider how natural selection has chosen the species which compose the ecosystem. This argument obviously needs much more evidence before it can be accepted; indeed, we shall now argue, equally conjecturally, in the opposite direction! But it reinforces our plea in Chapter 1, that ecologists should learn to walk – i.e. to study two-species relationships – before they run to attack whole ecosystems.

(5) A detailed study, during four consecutive seasons, of insects on alfalfa has left us with a distinct, but as yet unsubstantiated, impression that the 'stability' – however defined – of the ecosystem may depend on the successive appearances, through the season, of different species. If so, the workings of the ecosystem at any given time can still be described in terms of two-species behavioural interactions, but its functioning throughout the season would depend on the correct timing of successive arrivals; much as the development of an individual animal or plant depends on the timing of different genes acting in succession. There are several arguments leading in that direction. Populations of pea aphids on alfalfa in large field cages reached densities of 270 per plant terminal, whereas they rarely exceed 5 per terminal in the field outside. Yet the only noticeable difference between conditions inside and outside the cages was that the cages

excluded many species of predator (syrphid, chrysopid, anthocorid and nabid) which arrive during the course of the season. The cages did contain plenty of other natural enemies of aphids, notably coccinellids, parasites and spiders, but they did not stop the extraordinary increase in aphid numbers. We cannot argue that the cages prevented aphid emigration, because very few winged individuals were produced, either in the cages or in the field.

Working with another aphid and another parasite, Hughes and Gilbert (1968) showed that the natural rates of increase of aphid and parasite are such that the parasite would begin to overwhelm the aphid population if the season lasted any longer than it actually does. Hughes and Gilbert predicted that predator–prey oscillations would then begin, but that prediction is very dubious, since it relies on the crude 'random search' expression for the rate of parasitization (Chapter 4). Nevertheless, it is quite clear that the parasite's rate of increase does fit the normal length of season very well.

This argument is strengthened by the comparisons which we shall shortly make between the rates of increase of various aphids and their normal lengths of season (see Table 8.1): and by the fact that the temperature threshold for the development of aphids of a given species is higher in California than in British Columbia (Campbell *et al.* 1974), which means that the length of season in California, on the physiological time-scale, could be much greater than it actually is. These various arguments all point towards the notion of a succession of species, closely geared to the normal length of season. Current work on the insects associated with cotton in California should reveal whether this notion is merely a truism, or whether it is important to the 'stability' of the ecosystem.

(6) Even if an ecosystem is indeed no more than an assemblage of two-species behavioural interactions, there is still a serious difficulty. It takes at least one season to analyse one two-species relationship, and therefore something like $\frac{1}{2}n^2$ man–years to analyse all the relationships within an ecosystem of n species. Even if two species do not interact directly, that

fact must still be established. So the study of the half-dozen insect species associated with cotton in California takes us close to the limits of ecological complexity which can be analysed at present. According to Elton (1966), there are at least 3800 animal species in two square miles of English woodland, which would therefore take seven million man-years to analyse!

(7) These studies have emphasized the need for collaboration between ecologists with different skills – a collaboration which is possible only when each participant is convinced of its necessity. The difficulties of collaboration are greatest between the biologist and the mathematician. Although the mathematics involved is very simple, there are as yet few people capable of doing both the field work and the analysis successfully. Contrary to first expectations, it has proved easier to train field biologists in elementary mathematics, than vice versa.

The reason is that whereas the biologist is well aware of his mathematical incompetence, most mathematicians who enter the subject never participate in day-to-day data collection, and so never appreciate the critical importance of doing so; those that do, become overwhelmed by the complexity of field biology, so different from the simple elegance of formal mathematics. What the biologist takes for granted, therefore, comes as a complete surprise to the mathematician! If he is to be effective, the mathematician must keep his hands dirty by direct participation in the field work, so that the distinction between mathematician and field biologist disappears. The same is true in reverse for the field biologist; for as previous chapters have shown, the mathematical analysis itself often dictates what data shall be collected. Nobody has stated this absolute necessity, for the biometrician to be intimately acquainted with the data, more forcibly than the most successful mathematical biologist of all time, the late Sir Ronald Fisher: and as those who knew him can confirm, he often stated it very forcibly indeed!

It is therefore regrettable that a division of labour between mathematician and field biologist is so often taken for granted

What use is it?

(see, for example, the recent set of studies in quantitative ecology edited by Bartlett and Hiorns (1973)). An office-bound theoretician must either blindly accept whatever data the field worker offers him, or he must give orders for the collection of data, without that personal understanding of field work which comes only from direct and continuous participation, and not from mere visits of inspection. And field workers naturally resent being told that they are not competent to analyse their own data. We repeat, therefore, that the major problems confronting ecologists today are overwhelmingly those of field work, not of theory or analysis. Several examples in this book show that it is precisely the departures from simplistic theoretical assumptions which are important, and those departures can only be discovered empirically, in the field.

Ecological understanding

For lack of hard evidence, some of the arguments in the previous section were necessarily conjectural. Here it will be the same. Not enough case-histories have yet been studied for us to draw any broad generalizations. One difficulty is that we do not even know at what level of detail to look for such generalizations. But we can certainly point to areas where patterns are beginning to emerge.

(1) Campbell *et al.* (1974) and Neuenschwander (1975) have found that natural enemies of aphids have higher temperature thresholds, and longer generation times, than the aphids which they attack. This, they argue, ensures that parasite or predator attack cannot begin until the aphid population has begun to increase; only in exceptional circumstances can the predators catch up on, and overwhelm, the aphids. (By contrast, Frazer and van den Bosch (1973) have shown that a major reason for the economic success of the imported parasite, *Trioxys pallidus* (Haliday), in California is its ability to attack a large proportion of the first generation of walnut aphids – cf. Mackauer and van den Bosch (1973).) Similar patterns of temperature requirements have been found

for cotton and its specific pest species (Chapter 5), for cereals and their pests, for alfalfa and its pests and elsewhere. These patterns imply the existence of heavy selection against animals whose population numbers increase either too early or too late. Morris (1971) has notably confirmed that such selection occurs, in relation to emergence from hibernation. These very consistent differences between the temperature thresholds of ecologically-related species must be important, and it is possible that further comparisons of individual temperature requirements will tell us why. On the other hand, these temperature requirements, which specify the *timing* of population events, can be fully interpreted only when combined with reproductive and survival rates, which determine population *numbers*.

(2) Detailed analyses of predator–prey relationships have confirmed that many predators and parasites make no serious inroads into the numbers of their prey (Hughes and Gilbert 1968, Hassell 1969, Gilbert and Gutierrez 1973, Wratten 1973, Frazer and Gilbert 1976). Yet not every predator is so ineffective. The famous cases of *Rhodolia cardinalis* Mul. and *Cactoblastis cactorum* (Berg) (Doutt 1964) show that predators sometimes keep their prey at very low numbers over periods of many years. A similarly impressive case is that of a natural invasion by the chalcid *Blastothrix confusa* Erd., currently decimating the brown fruit scale *Parthenolecanium corni* Bouché in Russia (Saakyan-Baranova *et al.* 1971).

It is sometimes argued that predators and parasites can seriously reduce the numbers of their prey only when they are artificially introduced without their own natural enemies (Doutt 1964). That argument is self-contradictory, since if it were true, those natural enemies should themselves be ineffective in their native habitat. Admittedly, they sometimes are! But such arguments must, in any case, take into account the rate of increase per generation, and the number of generations per season, of which each species is capable. Hagen (1974) has shown that *R. cardinalis*, and several other effective predators of scale insects, have generation times far shorter than those of their prey – which is quite the reverse of the aphid predators mentioned above. We do not know why scale populations should support effective predators, while the aphid populations so far studied do not.

It is certainly not true that effective predators always have shorter generation times than their prey. Mrs Betty Lee informs us that in Australia, although *Typhlodromus (Metaseiulus) occidentalis* Nesbitt has a shorter generation time than its prey *Tetranychus urticae* Koch, it is not such an effective predator as *Stethorus vagans* (Blackburn), which has a longer generation time than *T. urticae*. The reason is that *S. vagans* can search the orchard trees much more thoroughly than can *T. occidentalis*. The effectiveness, or otherwise, of a given predator evidently depends not on any one factor, but on a combination of factors such as activity, voracity, temperature requirements, search pattern and generation time: but how these various factors combine to produce an effective predator is not understood (DeBach 1974). We may reasonably hope to obtain a realistic general theory of predation, once sufficient case histories have been studied in the field – and the methodology used in this book should be adequate to reveal that theory. There are, of course, technical difficulties in studying a really effective predator like *R. cardinalis*, since both it and its prey are always very scarce under natural conditions; but those difficulties are not insuperable.

(3) The same kind of comparison may be made between the aphid species themselves. Table 8.1 shows population parameters of four species of aphid. Despite the enormous aphid literature, these are the only four species for which all the parameters have been observed, on any given population. This fact in itself underlines the utility of population models, which require that *all* the relevant parameters be measured. There is no doubt that the parameters in Table 8.1 are adjusted to suit local requirements. For example, aphids in California have substantially higher temperature thresholds for development than their conspecifics in Vancouver. By reducing that threshold, they could increase the length of

season (measured on the physiological time-scale), were it
advantageous to do so (Campbell *et al.* 1974). Again, there is
no physiological reason to prevent increased fecundity in *M.
maxima*, since one host plant can support several aphid
families containing a hundred or more progeny in all. In fact,
the observed fecundity is optimal for the species (Gilbert and
Gutierrez 1973).

Table 8.1
Population parameters of four aphid species

	Macrosiphum rosae (L.)	Aphis craccivora	Masonaphis maxima	Brevicoryne brassicae
Location	South Australia	New South Wales	British Columbia	New South Wales
Host tissue	Rosebud	Medic plant	Thimbleberry terminal	Kale plant
Length of season on one host, day-°C	350	420	830	1100
Density-dependent control of fecundity	weak	weak	medium	strong
Maximum fecundity	120	95	54	38
Maturation time, day-°C	57	75	133	140
Source	Maelzer 1976	Gutierrez, Havenstein et al. 1974	Gilbert & Gutierrez 1973	Hughes 1963

A glance at Table 8.1 shows that different species are geared
to different circumstances. Ephemeral species with high
fecundity and rapid maturation time, living on ephemeral
hosts, go through one to three generations on one host and then
depart; while more sessile species, such as *B. brassicae*, can go
through several more generations on one host plant. Moreover,
the density-dependent control of fecundity, which reduces the

rate of population increase, acts strongly in *B. brassicae*, thus preserving the host plant for future generations of aphids: whereas the same mechanism is much weaker in the more ephemeral species, which therefore exploit the plant fully and rapidly. (Conversely, the ephemeral species produce a higher proportion of winged emigrants than does B. brassicae.) *M. maxima* lies between these two extremes. The differences between ephemeral and sessile species cannot be treated as a simple distinction between *r*- and *K*-selected species, for the various parameters interact in a complicated way, at least for *M. maxima* (Gilbert and Gutierrez 1973).

If Table 8.1 contained information on perhaps a dozen aphid species, we could try to generalize about the considerations which determine the values of the various population parameters. That is premature at present, because the number of relevant parameters – fecundity, body size, temperature threshold, and so on – exceeds the number of cases available. Here we must differ from Way and Cammell (1971) who have tried to draw such conclusions from even fewer species. Their argument rests on the relative strengths of the density-dependent mechanisms; by contrast, Kennedy and Stroyan (1959) consider generation time to be all-important. In fact, the population models insist that the various parameters are interlocked, and must be considered simultaneously. Once again, the models oblige us to consider all relevant parameters. Further population studies of this kind are therefore needed. The comparison of different populations offers a very suitable form of cooperation between ecologists, since each study is complete in its own right, yet contributes to the overall pattern.

(4) Another area in which population studies can give general understanding concerns the vexed question of ecological stability (Holling 1973, Hassell and May 1973). The obvious, classical definition of stability does not apply to the only detailed predator–prey relationship so far studied in the field (Chapter 4). Only further field studies can decide whether Holling's alternative notion of 'resilience' is meaningful. According to the theory of Chapter 3, resilience is

a by-product of natural selection acting in a different direction, so that questions of stability and resilience must be viewed as part and parcel of the larger problems concerning the genetical and ecological mechanisms of natural selection.

Practical utility

Earlier in this chapter, we argued that no approach to ecology can be considered successful, unless it gives useful recipes for practical manipulations in the field. This is not a question of economic advantage, but of assurance that we are thinking along the right lines.

It is still too early to decide whether detailed ecological analyses can be directly useful. At one extreme, Giese *et al.* (1975) propose that pest management should in future be controlled by state-wide computer networks. Such notions, we suggest, are premature. Giese *et al.* argue that, by accumulating daily increments of physiological time, we can monitor the development of a single-generation pest such as the alfalfa weevil and take action when the pest begins to damage the crop. But it does not take a computer network to sum increments of physiological time – an ordinary adding machine is just as good. Nor is it clear why, in such a case, control action must be delayed until the pest begins to damage the crop. At the other extreme, Way (1973) rightly says that detailed studies of individual case histories, even when dignified by names such as 'systems analysis' or 'life systems', have rarely resulted in practical recipes for management. The same is true of less sophisticated studies too. Time after time, ecological investigations have revealed how some pest was behaving, but have not revealed how to stop it! Frequently, the ecological study has completely overlooked some vital parameter. Sometimes, important aspects have proved impossible to study (Chapter 1). And only too often, no chink has appeared in the armour of some important pest. For these reasons, intensive ecological studies have contributed little to biological control or population management, which at present rely almost entirely on knowledge of the natural history alone. There is very little evidence to support the argument that, if we want more salmon, we should make intensive ecological studies of salmon.

The difficulty of producing recipes for control is hardly surprising. Of the hundreds of thousands of insect species, only two or three hundred rank as pests. They are pests because they are especially well adapted to take advantage of some particular circumstance engineered by man. Moreover, since physiological time depends on temperature (Chapter 2), it is impossible to predict the timing of population events in calendar time. That argument can be taken further. Where temperature has differential effects on two interacting species – so that low temperatures favour the prey, while high temperatures give the predator the upper hand (Chapter 4) – it is impossible to predict the precise course of events on any time-scale whatever, since events in a warm season must be different from those in a cool one. And sometimes, inappropriate weather conditions preclude the sampling of some species of animal, which again restricts practical applications in the field. There is therefore little immediate prospect that the methodology in this book can be used for direct, day-to-day pest management, simply because weather cannot be predicted. The gap between description and prediction is especially wide in ecology.

There is therefore good reason to argue that the distinction between ecologist on the one hand, and biological control worker or population manager on the other, will endure for some time; just as there is good reason to argue, conversely, that the distinction between mathematician and field ecologist must disappear. But increased understanding of population processes in general, and of the trade-off between one aspect and another in particular, can certainly help the practical manager. The same situation has already arisen in plant and animal breeding, where detailed genetical analyses have proved generally useless, but where genetical principles certainly guide the breeder's art. Already there are examples pointing the same way for population management:

(1) Parker and Pinnell (1972) successfully used a parasite to control numbers of the cabbage butterfly *Pieris rapae*. Having discovered that density-dependent effects restrict the parasite early in the season, they circumvented those effects by simultaneous mass releases of both pest and parasite. Their work certainly relies on ecological understanding, but not on any detailed prediction of the population dynamics.

(2) Croft and Thompson (1976) have derived empirical relationships to predict the numbers of predatory mites required to control a population of phytophagous mites in controlled conditions. Our own experience shows that such predation formulae vary with the temperature (Chapter 4), which must therefore be known first.

(3) Biological control has always been largely a 'try-it-and-see' affair, since laboratory studies designed to determine the potential effectiveness of some natural enemy can be grossly misleading. For example, detailed population studies show that the aphid parasite *Aphidius rubifolii* effectively lays about 90 eggs in the field, far less than the 400 observed in the laboratory (Mackauer and van den Bosch, 1973 and Chapter 10). So the effectiveness of some natural enemy can be evaluated only by detailed studies in the field (Hagen and van den Bosch 1968).

(4) All the studies made so far have emphasized that correct timing is critical to the outcome of control measures. Wilson *et al.* (1972) used a crude model of the cotton–insect relationship in Australia, to show that both planting dates and insecticide applications could profitably be delayed until fairly late in the season. That model has now been superseded by far more detailed work on Californian cotton (Chapter 5), which shows that pink bollworm damage can be reduced by a combination of irrigation and late planting which upsets the synchrony between bollworm and plant. In both cases, however, the farmers had already discovered the importance of correct timing by trial and error. But in future, both ecologists and

population managers will have to pay more attention to questions of timing.

(5) Studies of temperature requirements open up some interesting practical possibilities for biological control. As mentioned earlier, insect parasites and predators generally have higher developmental temperature thresholds than their prey. It seems reasonable to expect that laboratory-bred, or imported, natural enemies with lower temperature thresholds could prevent the natural build-up of pest populations at the start of the season. What would happen after that, we do not know. But biological control workers (e.g. van den Bosch and Messenger 1973) have often observed that successful, permanent introductions of parasites or predators into a given area generally come from regions of very similar climate. Therefore, there is considerable scope for detailed analyses of successful introductions, and for field experiments on animals with different temperature requirements. Rabinovich (1972) has begun laboratory studies on these lines.

(6) The detailed studies of insect behaviour, essential to any understanding of their population dynamics, can give direct rules for management. Thus the work on *P. rapae*, discussed in Chapter 6, shows that to minimize the number of eggs laid on your cabbages, you should plant the cabbages in very large, very dense stands, protected by a ring of widely-spaced plants around the edge to 'trap' most of the butterflies.

(7) Finally, we may mention two direct, practical applications of detailed population studies. Falcon *et al.* (1971) have shown that *Lygus* bugs cause far less damage to Californian cotton than was previously thought to be the case, and therefore demand far less stringent control measures. Regev *et al.* (1976) have used a cotton model to optimize the application of control measures, and to suggest taxation policies appropriate to the industry. This is an example of collaboration between ecologists and economists.

It is quite possible, however, that practical applications - as distinct from general understanding - will in future be based on ecological studies less detailed than those described in this book. Van den Bosch and Messenger (1973) have shown that, in certain cases, the success or failure of biological control has depended on very intimate details of adaptation or competition among the species concerned. If that argument is generally true, there is no immediate prospect of predicting the success of individual introductions, although there is a good prospect of understanding the general principles involved. The argument is strengthened by the unexpected failures mentioned in Chapter 7: but it is still insecure, simply because so few introductions have been studied in sufficient ecological detail to establish the reasons for their success or failure. On the other hand, the successful 'integrated control' programmes in Malaysia (Wood 1971) have relied on ecological studies which were far more detailed than is usual in biological control work, but much less so than those in this book. Again, Neuenschwander *et al.* (1975) have examined coccinellid predation of aphids on alfalfa over a wide area of California. As they themselves point out, their sampling methods are inaccurate (and we may now add in hindsight, heavily biased), and their assumptions about predator voracity are very questionable. Nevertheless, their data give a very broad picture of predation over a wide area, which may be just as useful in practice as a more accurate and detailed picture of events in one place.

Similarly, Wratten's (1973) study, although far from perfect (Chapter 4), does give a reasonable account of the true situation. Obviously, we should like to have fairly accurate studies, made over a wide area. The amount of work required is not prohibitive: for with a single season's work, Frazer, Gilbert, Ives and Raworth (unpublished) have extended the study of predation by adult coccinellids, discussed in Chapter 4, to cover the whole reproductive cycle, including the predation rate – and therefore the survival rate too – of larval coccinellids. At the same time, Dr P. M. Ives (unpublished) has measured the movements of adult ladybirds into and out of the field plots, as described in Chapter 6. Therefore, although the detailed studies in this book certainly take a lot of hard work, they can be done reasonably quickly and further experience should make them routine.

Our strictures in Chapter 1 were directed against laboratory ecologists who never venture into the field, and especially against theoretical ecologists who never venture into either the field or the laboratory. Dr Broadhead has pointed out that there are two schools of thought. First, there are those ecologists who (like us) believe that before we begin to theorize about ecological systems, we need to find out – at least in outline – how they actually work. The second school of ecologists wish to start with extremely simple theories, and elaborate them until they become realistic (Appendix). As mentioned in Chapter 1, we should have no quarrel with the second school, were they to test their theories *in the field*. That it is perfectly feasible to do so is a prime theme of this book. Meanwhile, ecologists have been distracted too often (or so we believe) by purely speculative theories, e.g. of predator–prey oscillations, Lotka–Volterra population dynamics, broken sticks and community matrices, which have later proved to be illusory.

In our experience, the most productive ecological studies are begun by choosing a suitable ecological relationship, and therefore species, to work on, according to the considerations of Chapter 2; and then observing that relationship with an open mind, uncluttered with theoretical hypotheses. The behaviour of the animals themselves will then raise a host of questions, and the whole art of the successful field ecologist lies in ignoring the unimportant questions; pursuing the important ones with meticulous attention; knowing when to stop; and recovering useful information from the inevitable failures. This description is obviously inadequate, for the choice between 'important' and 'unimportant' questions must evidently depend on the overriding question which the whole study is intended to answer. That question must certainly be posed as precisely and explicitly as possible: too many field studies, including some of our own, have given inconclusive results because the questions were ill-defined. But the field

88

ecologist is not like a mechanic dismantling a piece of machinery, or even like a mathematician exploring a new field of theory. He is far more like a detective, short-handed and racing against time, who is engaged in a battle of wits with the animals and plants themselves. That is what makes the subject so attractive.

One last point about practical utility. The human species has begun to overreach the limits of its environment. Ecologists are expected to provide the answers. In the present state of the subject, this is rather like trying to build dynamos with a science that is still at the iron-filings stage. But in any case, it is not the human species that is in danger of extinction, but many species of plant and animal. Any ecologist who is expected to produce results of economic value might well retort that his duty lies as much towards the animals and plants as to his own species. This argument does not, of course, excuse our present inability to predict events in the field.

Further outlook

To sum up, then, the approach described here does give some ecological understanding. It demands a new degree of rigour and coherence in field studies. It requires us to study all the relevant aspects and it promotes collaboration between botanists, zoologists, mathematicians and economists. Such specialists will inevitably be at cross-purposes, unless each participates in all aspects of the work. Although better understanding means better management, there is little prospect at present that realistic, detailed ecological models can prescribe day-to-day management.

Here we may mention a purely philosophical point. To be intellectually satisfying, a scientific explanation must refer some observed phenomenon to its antecedent causes at one or more levels of detail removed. Thus photochemical reactions are explained in terms of molecular orbitals, and nerve conduction in terms of ionic flows. For purely technical reasons, there are rather few areas of ecology where satisfying explanations of this kind seem to be feasible, at present. One is the explanation of population dynamics in terms of individual behaviour, and another is the explanation of plant and animal distributions in terms of biochemical and physiological requirements.

Given this entire situation, how should we proceed?

(1) There is a steadily growing need for field experiments on the manipulation of animal populations. The technique of this kind of experimentation is in its infancy (Chapter 7). Such experiments will be quite expensive financially, although much less so than current attempts to attack large ecosystems head-on. For purely political reasons, these experiments will probably have to use species of economic importance, even though other species might be preferable technically.

(2) The ultimate aims of ecologists must include an understanding of complete ecosystems. There is no reason why we should not analyse very small ecosystems containing half a dozen species. The effort required, although great, is not prohibitive.

(3) Further comparisons of different species, of predator-prey relationships, and so on, are needed. They could help to answer, if only partially, such questions as: What are the differences, if any, between pest species and innocuous species? Under what circumstances does a predator seriously, and permanently, reduce the numbers of its prey? What parameters decide the success, or otherwise, of new introductions?

(4) The methodology, modified as necessary, may be extended to suitable species of reptile, bird and mammal.

(5) We argued in Chapter 3 that the ecologist's task is to observe the products of natural selection, as they occur in real life. This will require analyses, both ecological and genetical, of chosen relationships in greater depth than has yet been achieved (cf. Ehrlich et al. 1975).

These various possibilities naturally overlap. At least they show that this approach to ecology is far from exhausted. We do not know whether it will cure our ignorance, but already we can echo Sir Joseph Banks, that 'it is however some pleasure to disprove that which does not exist but in the opinions of Theoretical writers' (Banks 1962).

PART 2

Introduction

This part of the book shows 'how the trick is done'. Chapters 9 and 10 describe, step by step, the construction of a simulation model, consisting of variable life-tables for an aphid and its parasite. This particular example is chosen because it is fairly simple, yet it illustrates many of the biological and technical questions that commonly arise. Starting with the field data, we deduce the various numerical or algebraic components of the model, and show how they are tied together to make a computer program. The same pieces of information therefore appear more than once, as field data, simple algebraic equations, flow charts or Fortran listings. This will enable one reader to grasp the gist of the biology very quickly, whereas another reader may wish to work carefully through every successive step in the argument. Chapters 9 and 10 are concerned solely with the transition from field data to computer model. The methods used to collect the data in the first place, and the conclusions eventually drawn from the model, appear in Part 1 and, in more detail, in a published paper (Gilbert and Gutierrez 1973): so they will not be repeated here. But various technical problems, common to all work of this kind, will be examined as they arise; and Chapter 11 will discuss some further technical points, peculiar to the other kinds of ecological relationship mentioned in Part 1.

9 AN APHID LIFE-TABLE

We shall analyse the ecological relationships between a host plant, thimbleberry (*Rubus parviflorus* Nutt.); an aphid, *Masonaphis maxima* (Mason); and its hymenopterous parasite, *Aphidius rubifolii* Mackauer. The basic natural history is given by Frazer and Forbes (1968) and by Gilbert and Gutierrez (1973). It will not be repeated here. This chapter is a first attempt to reproduce the population dynamics of the aphid. Chapter 10 will add in the parasites, and 'tune' the whole model until it reproduces the dynamics of both aphid and parasite. No model gives the right answer at the first attempt; Dr David Bennett has aptly remarked to us that 'the useful thing about a simulation model is to find out why it gives the wrong answer'. So we shall present six successive versions of the model, showing the changes made to reconcile the model to the field data. Sometimes these changes are compelled by biological information contained in the data, but overlooked until the model itself reveals its importance. Other changes are made purely empirically 'to give the right answer', in which case they betray our ignorance of the underlying biology.

The basic field data consist of a series of population samples taken throughout the season. The sample unit consisted of all the insects on one plant: the number of units per sample varied according to the aphid density. Averages for each sample appear in Table 10.5, or in Fig. 10.3. The aphids are sorted into their four juvenile instars and adults. Each age-group is further sorted into the various recognizable morphs: white sexual females, red sexual males, green wingless and winged parthenogens. The parasites are sorted into larvae and pupae. No records of the free-flying adult parasites are available. The field data also include the numbers of syrphid predators, not shown in Table 10.5. The insects on each plant within a sample were recorded separately, so that it is possible to calculate standard errors for each sample. These standard errors often exceed the value recommended in Chapter 7 of 10% of the mean. When aphids are scarce, high accuracy can be achieved only by samples which destroy an important fraction of the vegetation: when aphids are abundant, the sheer labour of counting and sorting them limits the sample size. But the field samples clearly reveal the pattern of events through the season, and our task is to reproduce that whole pattern.

The first step is to estimate the physiological time-scale, and to convert the basic field data to that scale. Physiological time-scales for the aphid and the parasite were estimated by growing aphids and parasites at several fixed temperatures in the laboratory (Campbell *et al.* 1974). Although the parasite's temperature threshold for development is higher than the aphid's, the difference is only 4°F. Strictly speaking, we should convert the daily maximum and minimum temperatures observed in the field to the corresponding amounts of physiological time for the aphid, using the aphid's temperature threshold (Chapter 2); and then do the same for the parasite, using the parasite's threshold. But since the two thresholds are very similar, the two physiological time-scales are nearly proportional throughout the season (except right at the start), and so in this case we may use the same time-scale for both species. This means that population events for both aphid and parasite, when measured on the same physiological time-scale, no longer depend on the ambient temperatures. Since the original paper uses the Fahrenheit scale, we shall express physiological time in day-°F, starting at the arbitrary origin of 1 May 1971.

The field data (Table 10.5) show that, at time 94 day–degrees, the first generation, or fundatrix, aphids have matured as green apterous adults and have started to produce second-generation progeny. The second generation begins to mature at time 204. There is a surge of births of third-generation first-instar aphids, including sexual forms for the first time, during 289–411. In subsequent samples, this third-generation surge appears in the second, third and fourth instars, and begins to mature at 587. The fourth generation, with a high proportion of sexuals, appears during 708–854 and becomes adult during 946–1090. The season ended abruptly at 1250, when a sudden heat-wave dessicated the host plants. The parasites went through two discrete generations, and were beginning a third when the season ended. This pattern, evident in Table 10.5, is even clearer when the data are drawn as histograms in Fig. 10.3.

Laboratory work shows that, on the physiological time-scale, the aphid requires roughly the same developmental period for each of its first three instars. That period, the same for every morph, is therefore a natural unit of physiological time, which we shall call one 'instar-period'. For *M. maxima* at Vancouver, it is 54 day-$°F$. The fourth instar then takes $1\frac{1}{2}$ instar periods for apterous (wingless) individuals, whether parthenogens or sexual females, and $1\frac{3}{4}$ for alate (winged) parthenogens and males. We therefore adopt a life-table with age-groups of one quarter-instar-period, or 'quip', so that the first three instars each take four quips, while the fourth instar takes six quips for apterous aphids and seven for alates. It is convenient to adopt the same unit – in this case, one quip – for both age and time, so that whenever time increases by one time-unit, every individual's age increases by one age-unit. (It would be possible, instead, to count age in quips and time in (say) half-quips, in which case each aphid's age increases by one unit at every *second* time-step; but this would complicate the program.)

We must therefore consider the very important question of how to choose an appropriate time-unit. The model works step-by-step, jumping from one time-unit to the next, rather like the frames of a cinema film. If the time-step is too long, the jumps will be too jerky, and the final numerical answers will consequently be distorted. If the time-step is too short, the program will use an excessive amount of computer time, and round-off errors may accumulate. It is therefore very important to choose an appropriate time-step. Some mathematical rules do exist, but they are generally unhelpful when applied to realistic ecological models. We therefore wrote a special version of the model, not shown here, which allowed the time-unit to vary from ¼ instar-period to 1/8, 1/16, 1/32. . . . This showed that one quip is a suitable time-step in the present case, since it returns answers much the same as those given by much shorter time-steps. It does not follow that one quip will be suitable for every population; for the faster a population changes in size, the shorter the required step-length. But in this case, one quip of $13\frac{1}{2}$ day-°F is appropriate.

The aphid's reproductive scheme is fairly complicated (Fig. 9.1). The overwintering eggs hatch in spring, producing the green parthenogenetic 'fundatrix' aphids which make up the first generation. The population is then maintained parthenogenetically for several generations by 'virginoparae' which are green in colour. Virginoparae give birth to aphids of three types: to further virginoparae, to 'gynoparae', and to sexual males. Gynoparae are green alate parthenogens which give birth only to the white sexual females, who mate with the males to produce overwintering eggs. So white aphids are sexual females, and red aphids are sexual males; while green

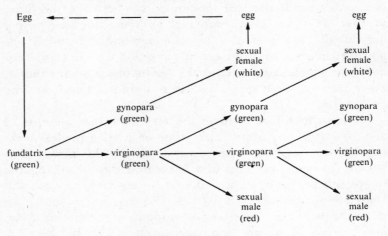

Fig. 9.1 Reproductive cycle of *M. maxima*.

aphids, if wingless, must be virginoparae, but if alate, may be either virginoparae or gynoparae. The presence or absence of wings may be recognized in the third and later instars.

Fig. 9.2 shows the average reproductive patterns of adult virginoparae kept at constant temperature in the laboratory. Each individual virginopara first produces all her green parthenogenetic progeny and then switches to producing red males; but a set of contemporary virginoparae produces the overlapping pattern shown in Fig. 9.2. That figure shows that

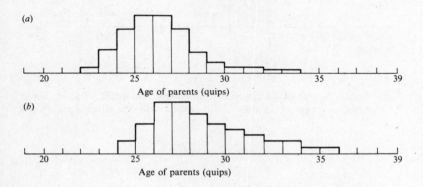

Fig. 9.2 (a) Age-pattern of production of parthenogenetic progeny by a set of contemporary virginoparae: values of REPAR in program. (b) Age-pattern of production of male progeny by same set of virginoparae: REMAL in program.

the aphids continue to reproduce between the ages of 23 and 36 quips, but then stop. When reproductive aphids are dissected, they always contain mature embryos; but post-reproductive aphids contain none. So if the aphids in the field always died before they finished reproducing, we should never find individuals with no mature embryos: but if the aphids lived a long time after they stopped reproducing, we should find many containing no mature embryos. From the proportion of adult aphids in the field samples, dissected and

An aphid life-table

found to contain no mature embryos, we deduced that on average, parthenogenetic aphids survive to age 40 quips. Fig. 9.3 therefore shows the life-history of an average aphid.

Although Fig. 9.2 shows the *pattern* of reproduction, it does not show how the actual *numbers* of progeny vary with time or

Instar	I	II	III	IV	V (adult) pre-reproductive	reproductive	post-reproductive
Age (quips)	1–4	5–8	9–12	13–18	19–22	23–36	37–39

Fig. 9.3 Life history of an apterous parthenogenetic aphid. If alate, instar IV extends over ages 13–19 quips, and adult events are all delayed by one quip.

with aphid density. In fact, the fecundity declines steadily through the season as the condition of the host plants deteriorates; and at any given time, the fecundity declines as the number of adults on the plant increases. This decline appears in Fig. 9.4 which shows the relationship between average fecundity (counting both the progeny already born and the unborn mature embryos) and number of adults per plant, in the second and third generations. In the first generation there were rarely more than one or two adult fundatrices per plant, while the fourth and fifth generations overlapped so much that we could not identify individual progenies. The exponential curves in Fig. 9.4 are fitted by regression, weighted according to the accuracy of the individual points. The absolute fecundity is lower in Fig. 9.4(*b*) than in 9.4(*a*), and the value of the exponent (0.0324 in

100

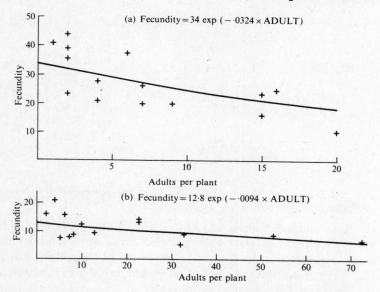

Fig. 9.4 Plots of observed average fecundity versus number of ADULTs. (*a*) second generation, (*b*) third generation.

(*a*), 0.00947 in (*b*)) changes in proportion. We therefore write the average fecundity as

$$A \exp(-\cdot 00096 \times A \times \text{ADULT}),$$

where ADULT is the number of adult aphids on the plant and A varies with time.

We may now estimate the values of A by correcting the fecundities observed in successive field samples for the changing numbers of adults per plant. In only eight samples, taken at appropriate times in successive generations, can we identify parents and progeny with any certainty. The results appear in Fig. 9.5. The absolute fecundity declined continuously throughout the season. Although the decline is undoubtedly due to the deteriorating condition of the host plants, we have no direct physiological information about the process, and so the value of A is quoted as a function of time, rather than of plant condition as such. We thereby assume that

An aphid life-table

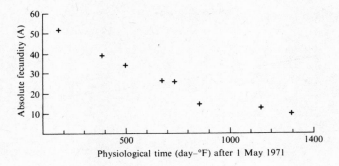

Fig. 9.5 Decline of observed absolute fecundity (corrected for density-dependence) through the season.

the same decline will occur – as indeed it does – every year. The value of A is taken to be a *linear* function of time. The decline might equally well be treated as exponential (Fig. 9.5), but in that case, although the numerical results are slightly different, the final conclusions remain the same.

We have now established the physiological time-scale, the average life-history of individual aphids and the reproductive rate. It is time to put these various pieces of information together to make a 'variable life-table' for the aphid (Table 9.1). Towards the end of the season, large numbers of dead aphids were observed in the samples, and we shall apply the corresponding survival rate, SURV, as an empirical function of time. There is no need to consider in detail how the formula for SURV was fitted to the data, because it will be replaced by an entirely different mechanism in Chapter 10.

Table 9.1

```
 1   C        PROGRAM MASONAPHIS  (FIRST VERSION)
 2            DIMENSION ALATE(40),APTRA(40),GYNOP(40),AMALE(40),FEM(40),
 3           *REPAR(14),REMAL(14)
 4            DATA REPAR/.02,.08,.16,.2,.2,.16,.08,.04,.02,.02,.01,.01,0.,0./
 5            DATA REMAL/0.,0.,.04,.1,.18,.18,.14,.1,.08,.06,.04,.04,.02,.02/
 6            WRITE(3,240)
 7        240 FORMAT(6H1 TIME,6X,7HAPHID I,9X,8HAPHID II,11X,9HAPHID III,14X,
 8           *8HAPHID IV,12X,11HAPHID ADULT/9X,2(17HWHITE RED GREEN   ),3(17HWHIT
 9           *E RED   GREEN,5X)/41X,3(13X,9HAPT ALATE)/)
10            DO 10 I=1,40
11            ALATE(I)=0.
12            APTRA(I)=0.
13            GYNOP(I)=0.
14            AMALE(I)=0.
15         10 FEM(I)=0.
16            APTRA(23)=.09
```

```
17          ADULT=.09
18          DO 1000 K=1,104
19          A=54.*(1.-K/104.)
20          REP=A*EXP(-.00096*A*ADULT)
21          PGYN=.35*(1.-((K-24.)/30.)**2)
22          IF(PGYN) 30, 40, 40
23       30 PGYN=0.
24       40 PMALE=(1.-PGYN)*(.0105*K-.092)
25          IF(PMALE)50,60,60
26       50 PMALE=0.
27       60 PARTH=1.-PGYN-PMALE
28          PAL=.7*(1.-K/104.)
29          EMBRY=0.
30          EM=0.
31          EF=0.
32          DO 100 I=23,36
33          X=ALATE(I+1)+APTRA(I)
34          EMBRY=EMBRY+X*REPAR(I-22)
35          EM=EM+X*REMAL(I-22)
36      100 EF=EF+GYNOP(I+1)*.5*(REMAL(I-22)+REPAR(I-22))
37          EM=EM*PMALE
38          EG=EMBRY*PGYN
39          EA=EMBRY*PARTH
40          I=39
41      140 ALATE(I+1)=ALATE(I)
42          GYNOP(I+1)=GYNOP(I)
43          APTRA(I+1)=APTRA(I)
44          AMALE(I+1)=AMALE(I)
45          FEM(I+1)=FEM(I)
46          I=I-1
47          IF(I) 150, 150, 140
48      150 APTRA(40)=0.
49          FEM(40)=0.
50          APTRA(1)=EA*REP
51          GYNOP(1)=EG*REP
52          AMALE(1)=EM*REP
53          FEM(1)=EF*REP
54          ALATE(9)=APTRA(9)*PAL
55          APTRA(9)=APTRA(9)-ALATE(9)
56          IF(K-62) 180, 180, 160
57      160 SURV=1.-(.0001425+(K-62)*.000003125)*(K-62)**2
58          SURV=SURV**.025
59          DO 170 I=1,40
60          ALATE(I)=ALATE(I)*SURV
61          GYNOP(I)=GYNOP(I)*SURV
62          AMALE(I)=AMALE(I)*SURV
63          FEM(I)=FEM(I)*SURV
64      170 APTRA(I)=APTRA(I)*SURV
65      180 GALV=0.
66          GAPV=APTRA(19)
67          RV=0.
68          WV=FEM(19)
69          DO 194 I=20,40
70          GALV=GALV+GYNOP(I)+ALATE(I)
71          GAPV=GAPV+APTRA(I)
72          RV=RV+AMALE(I)
73      194 WV=WV+FEM(I)
74          ADULT=GALV+GAPV+RV+WV
75          IF(K.EQ.7.OR.K.EQ.12.OR.K.EQ.15.OR.K.EQ.20.OR.K.EQ.21)GO TO 200
76          IF(K.EQ.26.OR.K.EQ.30.OR.K.EQ.35.OR.K.EQ.43.OR.K.EQ.52)GO TO 200
77          IF(K.EQ.63.OR.K.EQ.70.OR.K.EQ.81.OR.K.EQ.91)GO TO 200
78          GO TO 1000
79      200 GI=0.
80          RI=0.
81          WI=0.
82          GII=0.
83          RII=0.
84          WII=0.
85          GAL3=0.
86          GAP3=0.
87          RIII=0.
88          WIII=0.
89          GAL4=GYNOP(19)+ALATE(19)
90          GAP4=0.
91          RIV=AMALE(19)
92          WIV=0.
93          DO 190 I=1,4
94          GI=GI+APTRA(I)+GYNOP(I)
95          RI=RI+AMALE(I)
96      190 WI=WI+FEM(I)
97          DO 191 I=5,8
98          GII=GII+APTRA(I)+GYNOP(I)
99          RII=RII+AMALE(I)
00      191 WII=WII+FEM(I)
```

```
.01          DO 192 I=9,12
 02          GAL3=GAL3+GYNOP(I)+ALATE(I)
 03          GAP3=GAP3+APTRA(I)
 04          RIII=RIII+AMALE(I)
 05   192    WIII=WIII+FEM(I)
 06          DO 193 I=13,18
 07          GAL4=GAL4+GYNOP(I)+ALATE(I)
 08          GAP4=GAP4+APTRA(I)
 09          RIV=RIV+AMALE(I)
 10   193    WIV=WIV+FEM(I)
 11          A=13.5*K
 12          WRITE(3,250) A,WI,RI,GI,WII,RII,GII,WIII,RIII,GAP3,GAL3,
 13         *WIV,RIV,GAP4,GAL4,WV,RV,GAPV,GALV
 14   250    FORMAT(F6.0,2(2H *,3F5.1),3(2H *,4F5.1),3H **)
 15  1000    CONTINUE
 16          CALL EXIT
 17          END
```

OUTPUT FROM VERSION 1

TIME	APHID I			APHID II			APHID III				APHID IV				APHID ADULT			
	WHITE	RED	GREEN	WHITE	RED	GREEN	WHITE	RED	GREEN APT	ALATE	WHITE	RED	GREEN APT	ALATE	WHITE	RED	GREEN APT	ALAT
95.	0.0	0.0	2.9	0.0	0.0	1.2	0.0	0.0	0.0	0.0	0.0	0.0	0.0	0.0	0.0	0.0	0.1	0.0
162.	0.0	0.0	0.3	0.0	0.0	2.2	0.0	0.0	0.7	1.5	0.0	0.0	0.0	0.0	0.0	0.0	0.1	0.0
202.	0.0	0.0	0.3	0.0	0.0	0.4	0.0	0.0	0.9	2.0	0.0	0.0	0.4	0.8	0.0	0.0	0.1	0.3
270.	0.0	0.0	0.0	0.0	0.0	0.0	0.0	0.0	0.1	0.2	0.0	0.0	1.2	2.9	0.0	0.0	0.1	0.3
284.	0.0	0.0	0.0	0.0	0.0	0.0	0.0	0.0	0.1	0.1	0.0	0.0	1.0	2.7	0.0	0.0	0.4	0.3
351.	0.0	0.0	1.0	0.0	0.0	0.0	0.0	0.0	0.0	0.0	0.0	0.0	0.1	0.3	0.0	0.0	1.3	2.4
405.	3.8	1.7	28.2	0.0	0.0	1.0	0.0	0.0	0.0	0.0	0.0	0.0	0.0	0.0	0.0	0.0	1.4	3.
473.	14.0	9.5	41.5	6.6	3.3	39.7	0.2	0.0	1.1	2.3	0.0	0.0	0.0	0.0	0.0	0.0	1.4	3.
81.	1.8	2.0	1.3	6.6	6.0	10.2	14.0	9.5	14.8	26.7	6.8	3.4	14.4	28.7	0.0	0.0	0.8	2.
02.	0.6	0.2	2.0	0.1	0.1	0.1	1.1	1.3	0.3	0.4	10.3	11.7	6.6	16.6	17.8	8.1	26.9	45.
51.	14.4	12.9	8.9	11.8	8.4	11.9	3.4	1.7	4.4	1.9	0.3	0.2	0.6	0.4	29.3	21.0	33.7	62.
45.	4.3	5.6	1.2	9.8	10.5	4.3	15.0	12.6	7.9	2.5	11.1	7.2	10.3	4.2	23.1	19.5	20.5	43.
93.	0.9	10.2	6.9	0.9	2.1	1.7	2.3	3.5	0.4	0.1	10.0	14.9	2.9	1.1	29.8	20.5	20.5	7.
28.	0.0	26.5	3.8	0.1	29.3	8.0	0.6	17.1	7.7	0.8	1.3	5.9	3.7	0.5	39.8	36.0	21.7	7.

The first version of the Fortran program appears in Table 9.1. As the flow-chart (Fig. 9.6) shows, it is a very simple life-table; the only real complications are those imposed by the biology, namely the existence of five different kinds of aphid morph, and the formulae which specify the reproductive rates. The rest of this chapter will explain in detail how the program is written. Readers who do not wish to follow the Fortran in detail should therefore skip to Chapter 10, which describes how the parasites and the syrphid predators were added to the model. For a more *mathematical* treatment of the computational methods involved, see Streifer (1974).

The five kinds of aphid (Fig. 9.1) are called ALATE (green alate virginopara), APTRA (green apterous virginopara), GYNOP (green alate gynopara), AMALE (red sexual male) and FEM (white sexual female). Each may live to a maximum

Fig. 9.6 Flow diagram for Table 9.1 (see opposite).

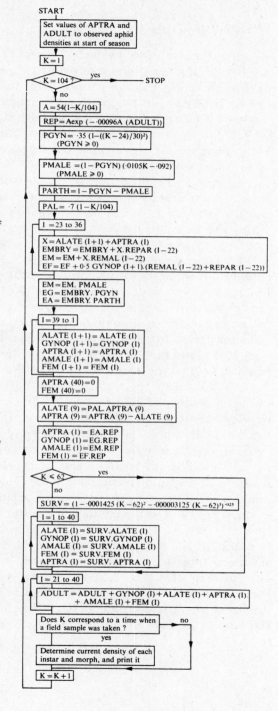

Set time clock to run from 1 at start of season, to 104 at end of season

Evaluate maximum potential fecundity (A) as a function of time, then evaluate REP by correcting A for the effects of aphid density

Evaluate PGYN, PMALE, PARTH, and PAL as functions of time

Determine total density (X) of adult virginoparae in each age class, and sum their reproductive capacities for male production (EM) and parthenogen production (EMBRY) Also sum reproductive capacity of gynoparae, which produce only sexual females (EF)

Evaluate overall morph proportions in this timestep's offspring

Age all aphids 1 QUIP, killing apterae and sexual females at age 40 QUIPS; other morphs die automatically at age 41 QUIPS

Divide newly-moulted third instar virginoparae into alates and apterae

Take previously calculated morph proportions, and multiply each by REP to obtain actual morph densities Put these offspring in age-class 1

Calculate survival rate during this time step; early in the season (K ≤ 62) survival rate = 1

Apply survival rate to all aphids

Determine total number of adult aphids now present, to be used in evaluating REP in the next time step

Book-keeping: compare the population structure and numbers predicted by the model with that observed in the field

Update time by one QUIP

Flowchart contents:

START

Set values of APTRA and ADULT to observed aphid densities at start of season

K = 1

K = 104 ? — yes → STOP

no

A = 54(1 − K/104)

REP = A exp (− ·00096A (ADULT))

PGYN = ·35 (1 − ((K − 24)/30)²) (PGYN ≥ 0)

PMALE = (1 − PGYN) (·0105K − ·092) (PMALE ≥ 0)

PARTH = 1 − PGYN − PMALE

PAL = ·7 (1 − K/104)

I = 23 to 36

X = ALATE (I+1) + APTRA (I)
EMBRY = EMBRY + X.REPAR (I − 22)
EM = EM + X.REMAL (I − 22)
EF = EF + 0·5 GYNOP (I+1).(REMAL (I − 22) + REPAR (I − 22))

EM = EM. PMALE
EG = EMBRY. PGYN
EA = EMBRY. PARTH

I = 39 to 1

ALATE (I+1) = ALATE (I)
GYNOP (I+1) = GYNOP (I)
APTRA (I+1) = APTRA (I)
AMALE (I+1) = AMALE (I)
FEM (I+1) = FEM (I)

APTRA (40) = 0
FEM (40) = 0

ALATE (9) = PAL.APTRA (9)
APTRA (9) = APTRA (9) − ALATE (9)

APTRA (1) = EA.REP
GYNOP (1) = EG.REP
AMALE (1) = EM.REP
FEM (1) = EF.REP

K ≤ 62 — yes →

no

SURV = (1 − ·0001425 (K − 62)² − ·000003125 (K − 62)³) ·025

I = 1 to 40

ALATE (I) = SURV.ALATE (I)
GYNOP (I) = SURV.GYNOP (I)
AMALE (I) = SURV. AMALE (I)
FEM (I) = SURV.FEM (I)
APTRA (I) = SURV. APTRA (I)

I = 21 to 40

ADULT = ADULT + GYNOP (I) + ALATE (I) + APTRA (I) + AMALE (I) + FEM (I)

Does K correspond to a time when a field sample was taken ? — no →

yes

Determine current density of each instar and morph, and print it

K = K + 1

age of 40 quips. For example, ALATE(I) is the current number of alate virginoparae of age I quips. REPAR and REMAL describe the age-pattern (Fig. 9.2) by which adult virginoparae give birth to green parthenogenetic and red male progeny. The values of REPAR and REMAL are quoted as DATA statements, lines 4–5 of the program (see Table 9.1). They are expressed as fractions: the values of REPAR all add up to unity, and so do the values of REMAL. The particular age-pattern of reproduction is important only when the population is rapidly increasing or decreasing (Fisher 1930): and the population size of *M. maxima* changes rapidly only during the first part of the season. So we did not investigate whether the age-pattern changes as the absolute fecundity declines, but assumed it to be constant. Gynoparae produce nothing but white sexual females, according to a time-pattern which is the average of the REPAR and REMAL patterns (line 36). If the time-pattern for gynoparae differed sharply from that of virginoparae, it would be quoted separately.

The program first sets all the aphid numbers equal to zero, lines 10–15, and then puts the number of fundatrices of age 23 equal to $0·09$ at the start of the season (line 16). Age 23 is the start of the adult reproductive period (Fig. 9.3), and the average number of fundatrices found in the early field samples was $0·09$ per terminal, which is rounded off to $0·1$ adult in the first two field samples taken at times 94 and 159 in Table 10.5. This argument will be modified in the next version of the model. Since the model represents an average plant terminal, these fractional numbers present no conceptual difficulty. The aphid season lasted 104 quips from the arbitrary time-origin of 1 May 1971, and so the model is set to run for 104 time-steps, line 18.

Lines 19–20 determine the level of fecundity at each successive time-step, i.e. at each value of K. Line 19 quotes the current value of A (Fig. 9.5). It declines from 54 at the start of the season ($K = 0$) to zero at the end ($K = 104$). Line 20 then applies the density-dependent effect (Fig. 9.4) as a function of the current average number of ADULT aphids per plant. It might be argued that it is not merely the adults, but also the young aphids, who compete for the food supply offered by the plant, so that the density-dependent effect should be expressed as a function of some unknown combination of numbers of aphids of all ages. But since, in practice, a given number of adults implies a given pattern of young throughout the generation, it is sufficient for our purpose to express the density-dependence as an empirical function of the number of adults only, even though the true biological effect may be more complex. This underlines the argument in Chapter 2, that the components built into a model need not reproduce the exact causal mechanism, provided that we do not overstep their limits of validity. In line 20, therefore, REP is the total number of progeny currently produced by one parthenogen, i.e. by one virginopara or one gynopara; it varies according to the time of season, K, and the density of ADULT aphids. The resultant progeny must next be divided into their various morphs.

The proportions of white, red and green aphids may be taken from the field samples (Table 10.5), but as explained previously, we cannot immediately distinguish green gynoparae from green alate virginoparae: the only detectable difference is that gynoparae produce white female offspring, while virginoparae produce green and red offspring (Fig. 9.1). Therefore, the proportion of gynoparae in any one generation is estimated from the proportion of females in the *next* generation. The formula for PGYN, the proportion of gynoparae among the progeny of virginoparae, is deduced by back-tracking in this way: it is calculated in lines 21-23 of Table 9.1. Once the proportion of gynoparae has been estimated, the proportions PMALE of males and PARTH of virginoparae may be found directly from the data, lines 24-27. Finally, the proportion PAL of alate individuals among the virginoparae is calculated in line 28. The formulae used to calculate these various proportions were all deduced directly from the appropriate plots of the field data. There is no need to consider in detail how the formulae were derived, because they will be changed in later versions of the model to correct for various kinds of bias caused by differential survival of the various morphs. Thus the formulae are purely empirical, being chosen to reproduce the true proportions of the identifiable morphs throughout the season. Once again, the changing proportions are calculated as functions of time K, because we have no knowledge of the biological mechanisms which determine them. But according to Fisher's (1930) theory, the ratio of sexual males to sexual females should be roughly 1 : 1 throughout the season – and so it proves to be in the final version of the model, but without any deliberate attempt on our part to make it so. This is a useful check, since the aphid's complicated reproductive scheme (Fig. 9.1) implies that the changing proportions of the various morphs must be delicately balanced to achieve a constant 1 : 1 sex ratio.

The next step is to combine all these aspects of reproduction to give the absolute numbers of progeny of different kinds. The whole calculation is based on a simple principle: multiply together the numbers of reproductive adults of both kinds (i.e. virginoparae and gynoparae) and various ages, the age-patterns of reproduction, the current individual fecundity and the current proportions of the four different morphs among the progeny. But the calculation is actually done in a different order, to enable the program to work as fast as possible. In lines 29–36, the program multiplies together the numbers of reproductive adults of different ages, and the time-fractions REPAR and REMAL, to obtain the *relative* amounts of reproduction during one time-step. It then adjusts for the current proportions of the various morphs (lines 37–39). EM, EF, EG, EA are therefore the *relative* amounts of reproduction of males, sexual females, gynoparae and virginoparae (both alate and apterous), during time-step K. When multiplied by the current individual fecundity REP, they give the actual numbers of young produced during one time-step (lines 50–53).

At each time-step K, the program promotes the life-table by one unit of age I, lines 40–47. For this purpose, it is necessary to start with the oldest age-groups and work downwards. For if instead we started with the youngest age-group and worked upwards, the numbers of aphids in each age-group would be overwritten and lost before that age-group had been promoted upwards. The loop is controlled by lines 40 and 47. In lines 48–49, apterae and sexual females die at age 40 (Fig. 9.3), while the other morphs simply disappear after age 40, because there is no aphid age-group 41. The program then uses the calculated reproduction to fill in the youngest age-group, lines 50–53. It also divides young parthenogens into alates and apterae, using the proportion PAL of alates calculated at line 28. The division is made at the beginning of instar III, lines 54–55, because the two morphs can first be distinguished at that age: and the formula for PAL is calculated accordingly.

Towards the end of the season, the program calculates the survival rate SURV, deduced from the proportions of dead aphids found in the field samples (lines 56–64). Since SURV is applied impartially to all 40 age-groups in lines 59–64, it is necessary to take the fortieth root of the observed value (line 58), so that the observed survival rate is achieved when SURV is applied 40 consecutive times to each cohort of aphids. This arbitrary survival rate will be eliminated when syrphid predation is added to the model in Chapter 10; but we shall always deal with survival rates, rather than mortalities, because we wish to keep track of animals which survive, not those that die. Next, the program sums all adults of various morphs (lines 65–73) to obtain the total current number of ADULTs (line 74), which is required for the calculations during the next time-step. If the time K has reached (to the nearest quip) the time of any one of the field samples (lines 75–77), the program adds up and prints the total numbers of the various instars and morphs for comparison with the field data. For example, GAL3, GAP3, RIII, WIII are the numbers of Green ALates, Green APterae, Red males and White females in instar III. The method of summation allows for the fact that winged morphs take seven quips to complete their fourth instar, while apterae take only six quips (Fig. 9.3).

One glance at the output figures in Table 9.1 shows that they are nothing like the field data in Table.10.5. Table 9.2 and Tables 10.1–10.4 show successive versions of the program, which correct the discrepancies one by one. They show the sequence of changes which was actually followed during the 'tuning' of the model. In each table, new or altered Fortran statements are marked with asterisks at the end of the line. It will be important to consider whether each alteration is biologically realistic and justified, or whether it is merely an arithmetic adjustment to 'give the right answer'.

In the output of Table 9.1, the second generation of aphids is far too discrete, and appears too late. In fact, the model predicts that the second-generation aphids will not reach their third and fourth instars until times 162 and 202 respectively and that there will be no first-instar aphids at all from time 202 to 284. So the start must be wrongly specified. Now the field records include, for each fundatrix observed, the number of progeny which she had already produced, found on the same terminal; and the number of mature embryos inside her, as determined by dissection. By comparing those two figures with the observed age-pattern of reproduction (Fig. 9.2), the age of each fundatrix could be estimated. The assumption made in Table 9.1, line 16, that all fundatrices were aged 23 at time $K = 0$, turns out to be wrong. Some fundatrices had begun to reproduce before $K = 0$. Therefore, the model has to start before its present origin of May 1.

If we shift the whole time-scale of K backwards, we should have to alter various Fortran statements involving K. Instead, the model is changed to permit negative values of K (lines 23–24, Table 9.2). The basic data also record that on some plant terminals there were young second-generation aphids, without the fundatrix who produced them. Some fundatrices had therefore been lost before the samples were taken, but they must be counted into the total number of fundatrices, which is thereby increased. This emphasizes the importance of getting a good fix at the start of the season, despite the difficulties of estimating a sparse population (Chapter 7). The numbers and age-distribution of fundatrices, estimated in this way from

Table 9.2

```
 1   C       PROGRAM MASONAPHIS (SECOND VERSION)
 2           DIMENSION ALATE(40),APTRA(40),GYNOP(40),AMALE(40),FEM(40),
 3          *REPAR(14),REMAL(14),FUND(23)                                    ***
 4           DATA REPAR/.02,.08,.16,.2,.2,.16,.08,.04,.02,.02,.01,.01,0.,0./
 5           DATA REMAL/0.,0.,.04,.1,.18,.18,.14,.1,.08,.06,.04,.04,.02,.02/
 6           DATA FUND/6*0.,3*.0028,4*.0056,2*.0084,.0112,.014,2*.0168,.014,  ***
 7          *.0112,.0056,.0028/                                              ***
 8           WRITE(3,240)
 9       240 FORMAT(6H1 TIME,6X,7HAPHID I,9X,8HAPHID II,11X,9HAPHID III,14X,
10          *8HAPHID IV,12X,11HAPHID ADULT/9X,2(17HWHITE RED GREEN  ),3(17HWHIT
11          *E RED    GREEN,5X)/41X,3(13X,9HAPT ALATE)/)
12           DO 10 I=1,40
13           ALATE(I)=0.
14           APTRA(I)=0.
15           GYNOP(I)=0.
16           AMALE(I)=0.
17        10 FEM(I)=0.
18           DO 20 I=1,23
19        20 APTRA(I)=FUND(I)                                                ***
20           ADULT=0.                                                        ***
21           DO 25 I=19,23                                                   ***
22        25 ADULT=ADULT+APTRA(I)                                            ***
23           DO 1000 KF=1,111                                                ***
24           K=KF-10                                                         ***
25           A=54.*(1.-K/104.)
26           REP=A*EXP(-.00096*A*ADULT)
27           PGYN=.35*(1.-((K-24.)/30.)**2)
28           IF(PGYN) 30, 40, 40
29        30 PGYN=0.
30        40 PMALE=(1.-PGYN)*(.0105*K-.092)
31           IF(PMALE)50,60,60
32        50 PMALE=0.
33        60 PARTH=1.-PGYN-PMALE
34           PAL=.7*(1.-K/104.)
35           EMBRY=0.
36           EM=0.
37           EF=0.
38           DO 100 I=23,36
39           X=ALATE(I+1)+APTRA(I)
40           EMBRY=EMBRY+X*REPAR(I-22)
41           EM=EM+X*REMAL(I-22)
42       100 EF=EF+GYNOP(I+1)*.5*(REMAL(I-22)+REPAR(I-22))
43           EM=EM*PMALE
44           EG=EMBRY*PGYN
45           EA=EMBRY*PARTH
46           I=39
47       140 ALATE(I+1)=ALATE(I)
48           GYNOP(I+1)=GYNOP(I)
49           APTRA(I+1)=APTRA(I)
50           AMALE(I+1)=AMALE(I)
51           FEM(I+1)=FEM(I)
52           I=I-1
53           IF(I) 150, 150, 140
54       150 APTRA(40)=0.
55           FEM(31)=0.                                                      ***
56           AMALE(31)=0.                                                    ***
57           APTRA(1)=EA*REP
58           GYNOP(1)=EG*REP
59           AMALE(1)=EM*REP
60           FEM(1)=EF*REP
61           ALATE(9)=APTRA(9)*PAL
62           APTRA(9)=APTRA(9)-ALATE(9)
63           IF(K-62) 180, 180, 160
64       160 SURV=1.-(.0001425+(K-62)*.000003125)*(K-62)**2
65           SURV=SURV**.025
66           DO 170 I=1,40
67           ALATE(I)=ALATE(I)*SURV
68           GYNOP(I)=GYNOP(I)*SURV
69           AMALE(I)=AMALE(I)*SURV
70           FEM(I)=FEM(I)*SURV
71       170 APTRA(I)=APTRA(I)*SURV
72       180 GALV=0.
73   C       (REST OF PROGRAM AS BEFORE)
```

OUTPUT FROM VERSION 2

TIME	APHID I			APHID II			APHID III				APHID IV				APHID ADULT			
	WHITE	RED	GREEN	WHITE	RED	GREEN	WHITE	RED	GREEN APT	ALATE	WHITE	RED	GREEN APT	ALATE	WHITE	RED	GREEN APT	ALAT
95.	0.0	0.0	1.3	0.0	0.0	2.4	0.0	0.0	0.8	1.7	0.0	0.0	0.2	0.4	0.0	0.0	0.1	0.0
162.	0.0	0.0	0.4	0.0	0.0	1.1	0.0	0.0	0.6	1.5	0.0	0.0	1.1	2.5	0.0	0.0	0.1	0.1
202.	0.0	0.0	0.1	0.0	0.0	0.6	0.0	0.0	0.4	0.9	0.0	0.0	1.2	3.0	0.0	0.0	0.5	0.7
270.	0.0	0.1	5.7	0.0	0.0	0.1	0.0	0.0	0.1	0.3	0.0	0.0	0.6	1.8	0.0	0.0	1.5	3.0
284.	0.1	0.3	10.7	0.0	0.0	0.3	0.0	0.0	0.1	0.2	0.0	0.0	0.5	1.5	0.0	0.0	1.7	3.4
351.	3.5	4.3	53.6	0.3	0.6	17.9	0.0	0.0	0.3	0.7	0.0	0.0	0.2	0.5	0.0	0.0	2.1	4.6
405.	8.4	8.2	52.0	3.5	4.3	53.6	0.3	0.6	5.5	12.4	0.0	0.0	0.3	0.8	0.0	0.0	2.3	5.0
473.	8.2	7.2	23.7	8.9	8.5	46.3	5.0	5.6	18.5	39.4	0.6	1.2	9.1	20.4	0.0	0.0	2.1	4.8
581.	1.8	1.3	3.5	5.1	4.3	9.0	8.2	7.2	8.5	15.3	12.1	13.1	25.2	61.3	2.4	2.1	18.4	30.8
702.	4.2	2.4	5.6	3.6	1.5	8.0	1.7	1.0	2.0	2.3	7.5	8.1	5.4	12.1	20.6	18.5	49.9	100.0
851.	4.7	4.5	2.5	3.7	3.0	2.5	3.9	2.6	2.5	1.1	6.1	3.3	5.8	5.8	11.9	9.0	45.0	93.9
945.	7.8	10.2	4.5	6.3	6.9	2.8	4.3	4.0	1.8	0.6	5.6	4.8	3.2	1.6	9.5	4.2	21.7	35.4
1093.	5.6	26.2	7.8	10.9	26.7	11.8	9.7	15.6	7.7	1.5	10.6	14.0	4.1	1.1	12.2	8.7	14.2	9.8
1228.	0.0	10.5	1.9	0.5	14.1	3.0	2.8	21.5	4.9	0.5	14.0	44.2	13.6	2.5	22.0	24.7	16.6	4.2

the field data, are inserted as a DATA statement in Table 9.2, lines 6–7. At the same time, we recognized that adult sexual males and females remain on the plant terminal for some time, and therefore appear in the samples; but then they move to the bottom of the plant (where the females lay their eggs) and so no longer appear in the samples. In Table 9.2, these sexual morphs are therefore eliminated from the model halfway through their adult life, at age 31, lines 55–56. We have no accurate estimate of how long these sexual morphs do, in fact, remain liable to sampling, and the age of 31 is chosen to give the correct, observed, ratio of sexual : non-sexual adults.

The basic aphid life-table is now complete. Most importantly, the timing of each successive generation is absolutely right. This would certainly not be true if we used calendar time instead of physiological time: for although the second, third and fourth generations each took about 300 day-°F to mature (Fig. 10.3), the calendar times were 23, 19 and 16 days respectively. But there are still many discrepancies between the output of Table 9.2 and the field data in Table 10.5. They will be resolved in Chapter 10.

10 APHID–PARASITE AND APHID–PREDATOR RELATIONSHIPS

This chapter shows how the effects of parasites and of syrphid predators are added to the aphid life-table (Table 9.2). Although the text will refer to the successive Fortran versions of the model shown in Tables 10.1 to 10.4, the broad outline of the argument may be followed simply by comparing the numerical output at the end of each table with the field data of Table 10.5. Fig. 10.3 compares the output of the final version (Table 10.4) with the field data in a different way.

The model has reached the stage of giving the correct timing for successive generations, but the aphid numbers predicted in Table 9.2 disagree profoundly with the field data (Table 10.5). There are far too many third-generation first-instar aphids during times 351–471. But the number of reproductive adults at that time is correct (even though the ratio of alate : apterous individuals is wrong), so the average fecundity must be too high. Yet the fecundity is estimated from the observed individual fecundity (Fig. 9.5) and the observed density-dependent effect (Fig. 9.4). The reason for the discrepancy appears in Fig. 10.1. As stated in Chapter 9, the model represents the density-dependent reduction in fecundity as an exponential function of the *average* number of ADULTs per plant terminal. But in real life, that reduction is determined for each terminal separately. Early in the season, a few terminals carry several adult aphids, while most have none at all. The effect of density-dependence on those terminals which bear some aphids is therefore much more severe than that calculated by the model. The trouble arises because the density-dependent effect is not linear, but exponential.

Fig. 10.1 was calculated as follows. For each individual plant terminal in one field sample, the value of the overall fecundity was calculated for the total number of adult aphids

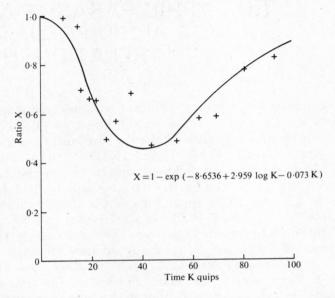

$$X = 1 - \exp\left(-8 \cdot 6536 + 2 \cdot 959 \log K - 0 \cdot 073\,K\right)$$

Fig. 10.1 Ratios of average numbers of aphid progeny, computed for individual plants in each sample, to average numbers of aphid progeny, as computed in the model from sample averages. See text for detailed explanation. Successive points refer to successive samples.

found on that terminal. The average, taken over all plants in the sample, of these fecundities is the value that ought to be used in the model. That average was compared with the value actually used in the model, which is calculated from the average number of adults per plant. The ratios, calculated in this way for successive field samples, appear in Fig. 10.1. This purely statistical effect is clearly important – i.e. the ratio differs considerably from unity – early in the season. There are two ways of correcting the discrepancy. One is to elaborate the model to include a distribution of aphids-per-terminal and calculate the fecundity for each terminal separately. There is no point in doing so, because we do not know how the distribution would change in response to changing circumstances; so we can only assume that the ratios, whose calculated values are shown in Fig. 10.1, will behave in the same way every year, even though the actual numbers of aphids may vary to some extent. In that case, the simplest method of correction is to multiply the fecundity, as computed in the model, by the appropriate ratio X from Fig. 10.1 (lines 26–32 of Table 10.1). The expression for X is found by fitting a suitable curve to Fig. 10.1 by non-linear regression. The value of X is quoted as a function of time K, rather than of the average number of ADULTs, because it corrects for the changing distribution of aphids, not for changes in average aphid density. The correction is important only during the first two generations, after which time the aphids have spread out over the plants. So the model now assumes that the aphids will spread out, to infest all available plants, every season – as indeed they do.

Table 10.1

```
 1  C       PROGRAM MASONAPHIS (THIRD VERSION)
 2          DIMENSION ALATE(40),APTRA(40),GYNOP(40),AMALE(40),FEM(40),
 3         *REPAR(14),REMAL(14),FUND(23)
 4          DATA REPAR/.02,.08,.16,.2,.2,.16,.08,.04,.02,.02,.01,.01,0,.0/
 5          DATA REMAL/0.,0.,.04,.1,.18,.18,.14,.1,.08,.06,.04,.04,.02,.02/
 6          DATA FUND/6*0.,3*.0028,4*.0056,2*.0084,.0112,.014,2*.0168,.014,
 7         *.0112,.0056,.0028/
 8          WRITE(3,240)
 9      240 FORMAT(6H1 TIME,6X,7HAPHID J,9X,8HAPHID II,11X,9HAPHID III,14X,
10         *8HAPHID IV,12X,11HAPHID ADULT/9X,2(17HWHITE RED GREEN  ),3(17HWHIT
11         *E RED  GREEN,5X)/41X,3(13X,9HAPT ALATE)/)
12          DO 10 I=1,40
13          ALATE(I)=0.
14          APTRA(I)=0.
15          GYNOP(I)=0.
16          AMALE(I)=0.
17       10 FEM(I)=0.
18          DO 20 I=1,23
19       20 APTRA(I)=FUND(I)
20          ADULT=0.
21          DO 25 I=19,23
22       25 ADULT=ADULT+APTRA(I)
23          DO 1000 KF=1,111
24          K=KF-10
25          A=54.*(1.-K/104.)
26          IF(K) 26, 26, 27
27       26 X=1.                                                      ***
28          GO TO 28                                                  ***
29       27 X=K                                                       ***
30          X=-8.6536+2.959*ALOG(X)-.073*X                            ***
31          X=1.-EXP(X)                                               ***
32       28 REP=A*EXP(-.00096*A*ADULT)*X
33          PGYN=.35*(1.-((K-24.)/30.)**2)
34          IF(PGYN) 30, 40, 40
35       30 PGYN=0.
36       40 PMALE=(1.-PGYN)*(.0105*K-.092)
37          IF(PMALE)50,60,60
38       50 PMALE=0.
39       60 PARTH=1.-PGYN-PMALE
40          PAL=.7*(1.-K/104.)
41          EMBRY=0.
42          FM=0.
43          FF=0.
```

```
44          DO 100 I=23,36
45          X=ALATE(I+1)+APTRA(I)
46          EMBRY=EMBRY+X*REPAR(I-22)
47          EM=EM+X*REMAL(I-22)
48   100    EF=EF+GYNOP(I+1)*.5*(REMAL(I-22)+REPAR(I-22))
49          EM=EM*PMALE
50          EG=EMBRY*PGYN
51          EA=EMBRY*PARTH
52          I=39
53   140    ALATE(I+1)=ALATE(I)
54          GYNOP(I+1)=GYNOP(I)
55          APTRA(I+1)=APTRA(I)
56          AMALE(I+1)=AMALE(I)
57          FEM(I+1)=FEM(I)
58          I=I-1
59          IF(I) 150, 150, 140
60   150    APTRA(40)=0.
61          FEM(31)=0.
62          AMALE(31)=0.
63          APTRA(1)=EA*REP
64          GYNOP(1)=EG*REP
65          AMALE(1)=EM*REP
66          FEM(1)=EF*REP
67          ALATE(9)=APTRA(9)*PAL
68          APTRA(9)=APTRA(9)-ALATE(9)
69          IF(K-62) 180, 180, 160
70   160    SURV=1.-(.0001425*(K-62)*.000003125)*(K-62)**2
71          SURV=SURV**.025
72          DO 170 I=1,40
73          ALATE(I)=ALATE(I)*SURV
74          GYNOP(I)=GYNOP(I)*SURV
75          AMALE(I)=AMALE(I)*SURV
76          FEM(I)=FEM(I)*SURV
77   170    APTRA(I)=APTRA(I)*SURV
78   180    GALV=0.
79   C      (REST OF PROGRAM AS BEFORE)
```

OUTPUT FROM VERSION 3

TIME	APHID I			APHID II			APHID III				APHID IV				APHID ADULT			
	WHITE	RED	GREEN	WHITE	RED	GREEN	WHITE	RED	GREEN APT	ALATE	WHITE	RED	GREEN APT	ALATE	WHITE	RED	GREEN APT	ALATE
95.	0.0	0.0	1.3	0.0	0.0	2.4	0.0	0.0	0.8	1.7	0.0	0.0	0.2	0.4	0.0	0.0	0.1	0.0
162.	0.0	0.0	0.4	0.0	0.0	1.1	0.0	0.0	0.6	1.4	0.0	0.0	1.1	2.5	0.0	0.0	0.5	0.7
202.	0.0	0.0	0.1	0.0	0.0	0.5	0.0	0.0	0.4	0.9	0.0	0.0	1.2	3.0	0.0	0.0	1.5	3.0
270.	0.0	0.1	4.1	0.0	0.0	0.1	0.0	0.0	0.1	0.3	0.0	0.0	0.6	1.8	0.0	0.0	1.7	3.4
284.	0.1	0.2	7.6	0.0	0.0	0.3	0.0	0.0	0.2	0.2	0.0	0.0	0.5	1.5	0.0	0.0	2.1	4.6
351.	2.2	2.7	33.3	0.2	0.4	12.4	0.0	0.0	3.8	8.6	0.0	0.0	0.3	0.6	0.0	0.0	2.2	5.0
405.	4.7	4.6	29.3	2.2	2.7	33.3	0.2	0.4	4.2	8.6	0.0	0.0	0.3	0.6	0.0	0.0	2.0	4.7
473.	4.1	3.6	11.9	4.9	4.6	25.4	3.0	3.4	11.2	23.9	0.0	0.8	6.1	13.8	0.0	0.0	2.0	4.7
581.	0.9	0.7	1.7	2.4	2.0	4.2	4.1	3.6	4.2	7.7	6.8	7.4	14.2	35.2	1.5	1.4	12.1	20.9
702.	8.1	4.6	10.3	3.8	1.6	7.9	1.0	0.5	1.1	1.3	3.6	3.9	2.5	5.8	11.3	10.4	29.4	59.5
851.	8.7	8.4	4.4	9.5	7.8	6.2	9.7	6.6	6.1	2.7	9.0	4.8	8.1	7.0	6.1	4.5	24.9	52.6
945.	5.0	6.4	3.1	7.8	8.4	3.4	8.9	8.2	3.6	1.1	14.6	12.5	8.0	4.0	12.8	5.4	17.4	22.0
1093.	4.0	22.3	8.1	6.3	16.4	9.2	4.9	7.8	4.9	1.0	9.5	13.2	3.5	1.1	27.6	20.5	23.2	13.1
1228.	0.0	15.6	2.3	0.5	19.5	4.0	2.2	21.9	5.8	0.6	8.5	28.7	11.4	2.0	17.9	19.8	20.0	6.6

The numbers of aphids are now quite reasonable up to the third generation (Table 10.1), but the proportion of alates among the juvenile green aphids is too low early in the season and too high towards the end. The initial estimate of PAL, the proportion of alates among the virginoparae, is unavoidably biased, because it counts in the gynoparae, which cannot be distinguished from alate virginoparae. Table 10.2 therefore alters the expression for PAL to give the correct proportions of alates. The new expression is found by trial and error.

Table 10.2

```
 1  C       PROGRAM MASONAPHIS (FOURTH VERSION)
 2          DIMENSION ALATE(40),APTRA(40),GYNOP(40),AMALE(40),FEM(40),
 3         *REPAR(14),REMAL(14),FUND(23),TN(120)                              ***
 4          DATA REPAR/.02,.08,.16,.2,.2,.16,.08,.04,.02,.02,.01,.01,0.,0./
 5          DATA REMAL/0.,0.,.04,.1,.18,.18,.14,.1,.08,.06,.04,.04,.02,.02/
 6          DATA FUND/6*0.,3*.0028,4*.0056,2*.0084,.0112,.014,2*.0168,.014,
 7         *.0112,.0056,.0028/
 8          WRITE(3,240)
 9      240 FORMAT(6H1 TIME,6X,7HAPHID I,9X,8HAPHID II,11X,9HAPHID III,14X,
10         *8HAPHID IV,12X,11HAPHID ADULT/9X,2(17HWHITE RED GREEN ),3(17HWHIT
11         *E RED   GREEN,5X)/41X,3(13X,9HAPT ALATE)/)
12          DO 10 I=1,40
13          ALATE(I)=0.
14          APTRA(I)=0.
15          GYNOP(I)=0.
16          AMALE(I)=0.
17       10 FEM(I)=0.
18          DO 20 I=1,23
19       20 APTRA(I)=FUND(I)
20          ADULT=0.
21          DO 25 I=19,23
22       25 ADULT=ADULT+APTRA(I)
23          DO 1000 KF=1,111
24          K=KF-10
25          A=54.*(1.-K/104.)
26          IF(K) 26, 26, 27
27       26 X=1.
28          GO TO 28
29       27 X=K
30          X=-8.6536+2.959*ALOG(X)-.073*X
31          X=1.-EXP(X)
32       28 REP=A*EXP(-.00096*A*ADULT)*X
33          PGYN=.35*(1.-((K-24.)/30.)**2)
34          IF(PGYN) 30, 40, 40
35       30 PGYN=0.
36       40 PMALE=(1.-PGYN)*(.0105*K-.092)
37          IF(PMALE)50,60,60
38       50 PMALE=0.
39       60 PARTH=1.-PGYN-PMALE
40          PAL=.44-.01*K
41          IF(PAL) 65, 65, 70                                               ***
42       65 PAL=0.                                                           ***
43       70 EMBRY=0.                                                         ***
44          EM=0.                                                            ***
45          EF=0.
46          DO 100 I=23,36
47          X=ALATE(I+1)+APTRA(I)
48          EMBRY=EMBRY+X*REPAR(I-22)
49          EM=EM+X*REMAL(I-22)
50      100 EF=EF+GYNOP(I+1)*.5*(REMAL(I-22)+REPAR(I-22))
51          EM=EM*PMALE
52          EG=EMBRY*PGYN
53          EA=EMBRY*PARTH
54          I=39
55      140 ALATE(I+1)=ALATE(I)
56          GYNOP(I+1)=GYNOP(I)
57          APTRA(I+1)=APTRA(I)
58          AMALE(I+1)=AMALE(I)
59          FEM(I+1)=FEM(I)
60          I=I-1
61          IF(I) 150, 150, 140
62      150 APTRA(40)=0.
63          FEM(31)=0.
64          AMALE(31)=0.
65          APTRA(1)=EA*REP
66          GYNOP(1)=EG*REP
```

Aphid-parasite and aphid-predator relationships

```
67          AMALE(1)=EM*REP
68          FEM(1)=EF*REP
69          ALATE(9)=APTRA(9)*PAL
70          APTRA(9)=APTRA(9)-ALATE(9)
71          TOT=0.
72          DO 152 I=1,40
73      152 TOT=TOT+ALATE(I)+APTRA(I)+GYNOP(I)+AMALE(I)+FEM(I)
74          TN(KF)=TOT
75          PRED=0.
76          IF(K-30) 310, 310, 301
77      301 JS=K-39
78          IF(JS) 302, 302, 303
79      302 JS=1
80      303 JF=K-30
81          DO 304 I=JS,JF
82      304 PRED=PRED+TN(I)
83          PRED=PRED*2.5
84      310 IF(K-20) 320, 320, 311
85      311 JS=K-29
86          IF(JS) 312,312,313
87      312 JS=1
88      313 JF=K-20
89          DO 314 I=JS,JF
90      314 PRED=PRED+TN(I)
91          PRED=PRED*3.
92      320 IF(K-10) 330, 330, 321
93      321 JS=K-19
94          IF(JS) 322, 322, 323
95      322 JS=1
96      323 JF=K-10
97          DO 324 I=JS,JF
98      324 PRED=PRED+TN(I)
99          PRED=PRED*2.
100     330 IF(K) 340, 340, 331
101     331 JS=K-9
102         IF(JS) 332, 332, 333
103     332 JS=1
104     333 JF=K
105         DO 334 I=JS,JF
106     334 PRED=PRED+TN(I)
107     340 PRED=.0001*PRED
108         SURV=EXP(-PRED/TOT)
109         IF(K-35) 180, 180, 155
110     155 ALATE(21)=ALATE(21)*.36
111         GYNOP(21)=GYNOP(21)*.36
112         APTRA(20)=APTRA(20)*.65
113     180 DO 170 I=1,40
114         ALATE(I)=ALATE(I)*SURV
115         GYNOP(I)=GYNOP(I)*SURV
116         AMALE(I)=AMALE(I)*SURV
117         FEM(I)=FEM(I)*SURV
118     170 APTRA(I)=APTRA(I)*SURV
119         GALV=0.
120   C     (REST OF PROGRAM AS BEFORE)
```

OUTPUT FROM VERSION 4

TIME	APHID I WHITE	RED	GREEN	APHID II WHITE	RED	GREEN	APHID III WHITE	RED	GREEN APT	ALATE	APHID IV WHITE	RED	GREEN APT	ALATE	APHID ADULT WHITE	RED	GREEN APT	ALATE
95. *	0.0	0.0	1.3 *	0.0	0.0	2.4 *	0.0	0.0	1.4	1.0 *	0.0	0.0	1.9	1.5 *	0.0	0.0	0.1	0.0
162. *	0.0	0.0	0.4 *	0.0	0.0	1.1 *	0.0	0.0	1.2	0.9 *	0.0	0.0	1.9	1.9 *	0.0	0.0	0.9	0.4
202. *	0.0	0.0	0.1 *	0.0	0.0	0.6 *	0.0	0.0	0.7	0.6 *	0.0	0.0	1.1	1.2 *	0.0	0.0	2.7	1.9
270. *	0.0	0.1	5.0 *	0.0	0.0	0.1 *	0.0	0.0	0.2	0.2 *	0.0	0.0	0.9	1.0 *	0.0	0.0	3.0	2.1
284. *	0.1	0.2	8.8 *	0.0	0.0	0.4 *	0.0	0.0	0.1	0.1 *	0.0	0.0	0.2	0.3 *	0.0	0.0	3.8	2.9
351. *	2.2	2.8	34.3 *	0.2	0.5	14.0 *	0.0	0.0	0.5	0.5 *	0.0	0.0	0.6	0.5 *	0.0	0.0	4.0	3.2
405. *	4.7	4.6	28.4 *	2.2	2.8	34.3 *	0.2	0.5	7.4	6.6 *	0.0	0.0	0.6	0.5 *	0.0	0.0	3.7	3.0
473. *	4.1	3.5	11.3 *	4.8	4.6	24.4 *	2.9	3.5	19.2	16.2 *	0.0	0.9	11.7	10.5 *	0.0	0.0	3.5	2.6
581. *	0.8	0.7	1.9 *	2.4	1.9	3.8 *	4.1	3.4	6.7	4.5 *	6.6	7.4	23.3	22.7 *	1.5	1.5	16.4	8.6
702. *	7.9	8.5	17.6 *	2.8	2.6	11.2 *	0.7	0.6	1.9	0.8 *	3.5	3.6	3.7	3.1 *	10.8	10.1	32.3	14.8
851. *	7.7	12.2	6.3 *	9.6	13.4	10.1 *	9.8	11.9	14.4	0.5 *	7.6	7.9	17.8	4.2 *	5.2	4.0	25.2	11.4
945. *	2.3	5.0	2.9 *	5.1	8.9	3.5 *	7.7	11.9	6.7	0.0 *	13.9	20.6	17.4	0.5 *	10.2	7.9	21.6	4.4
1093. *	1.8	19.5	7.2 *	2.6	13.3	7.9 *	1.8	5.7	4.9	0.0 *	4.4	10.5	3.5	0.0 *	20.9	26.8	26.0	1.5
1228. *	0.0	11.4	1.5 *	0.2	15.5	3.1 *	0.9	16.6	4.9	0.0 *	3.0	19.7	9.4	0.0 *	7.2	13.2	15.7	0.1

118

Incidentally, since PAL becomes zero after time 44 quips or 600 day-°F, all green alates produced during the second half of the season must have been gynoparae. This makes biological sense, since there would be no point in producing alate virginoparae once all the host plants had been colonized.

Another defect of Table 10.1 is that after time 400, the predicted numbers of instar IV aphids are about right, but the numbers of adults (which those aphids subsequently become) are much too high. Comparisons of the IV instar : adult ratios in the model, and in the data, reveal deficiencies of 35% in adult apterae and 64% in adult alates. The comparisons can be made only with the aid of a simulation model, because they are complicated by the different time-spans, and the rapidly changing aphid numbers, in the two stages concerned. These losses cannot be investigated directly in the field, but they presumably occur when the young adults migrate to fresh host plants: much heavier losses of migrants, and especially of alate migrants, are known in other species of aphid. So Table 10.2 applies the corresponding survival rates at the time when newly-mature adults migrate to fresh plants, lines 109–112. These survival rates are used to 'give the right answer'. We do not know how they might vary as circumstances change; but the method of estimation is very reputable, because it directly compares the size of the same cohort of animals at successive times.

Table 10.2 also introduces the syrphid predators for the first time. It would be useless to correct the aphid numbers any further until the syrphids are represented, because syrphid predation becomes important towards the end of the season. We know far too little about the detailed dynamics of the syrphid population, or of the predation process itself, to construct a realistic syrphid life-table. But we know that the adult hoverflies lay their eggs on plants which bear aphids. We know, from the field records, how many syrphid larvae were present. We know, from laboratory studies, the developmental time of syrphid larvae and their voracity at different ages.

Therefore, in Table 10.2, the model is amended as follows.

Aphid-parasite and aphid-predator relationships

Syrphid eggs are laid in proportion to the total number of aphids currently on the terminal. These syrphid larvae go through four developmental periods ('instars'), each lasting ten quips. The voracities of those four 'instars' are 1, 2, 6 and 15 average-sized aphids per quip, giving the total (observed) consumption of 240 aphids per syrphid. Now a 'first-instar' syrphid could have hatched at any time during the previous ten quips. So if TN(I) is the total number of aphids present on the terminal at time I, and if the number of syrphid eggs which are laid at time I is proportional to TN(I), the number of 'first-instar' syrphid larvae present at time K will be proportional to the sum of TN(I) from I = K−9 to I = K. Similarly the number of 'second-instar' syrphids will be proportional to the sum of TN(I) from I = K−19 to I = K−10: and so on. The constant of proportionality is intended to give the numbers of syrphid larvae actually observed in the field. The model would, of course, be simpler if it merely quoted those observed numbers of larvae, rather than generate them anew. But by making syrphid numbers proportional to aphid numbers, we allow the syrphids to respond to changes in aphid numbers, as they do in reality. So the model calculates the total demand per time-step, PRED, of syrphid larvae for aphids (lines 75–107) from past values of TN(I) which it has stored at each previous time-step (lines 71–74). It then calculates the predation rate, or rather the survival rate, of the aphids, assuming that the syrphid larvae search for, and find, aphids at random; the survival rate used in line 108 is therefore the Thompson exponential derived in Chapter 4. This representation would doubtless be far too crude if the relationship between syrphids and aphids were of primary interest; but in this case, it proves to be good enough as a peripheral survival rate affecting the plant–aphid–parasite relationship. Syrphid predation, so calculated, accounts for all the aphid corpses observed in the later field samples, and so the old survival rate, SURV, is now discarded in favour of the syrphids.

Table 10.2 gives answers which, although not perfect, are of the right order throughout. In particular, the timing of the generations and the proportions of the different morphs are realistic. It is therefore time to set up a life-table for the parasites. The laboratory data show that parasite survival does not depend on the age, or morph, of the aphid host. If it did, we should have to record parasite numbers in a two-way table, to specify the ages of both host and parasite simultaneously. But in this case, a single life-table may be used for the parasite. Fig. 10.2 shows the parasite's life-history, as revealed by

Stage	egg	larva	pupa	adult
age (quips)	1–6	7–23	24–34	35–52

Fig. 10.2 Life-history of *Aphidius rubifolii*.

laboratory studies. The next paragraph will describe in detail how the parasite life-table is built into the Fortran program in Table 10.3, and how it is used to determine the rate of aphid parasitization, assuming 'random search'.

In Table 10.3, PAR(I) is the current number of parasites of age I quips. PAREG(I) records the average number of eggs per

Table 10.3

```
 1  C      PROGRAM MASONAPHIS - APHIDIUS (FIFTH VERSION)
 2         DIMENSION ALATE(40),APTRA(40),GYNOP(40),AMALE(40),FEM(40),
 3        *REPAR(14),REMAL(14),FUND(23),TN(120),PAR(52),PAREG(52)          ***
 4         DATA REPAR/.02,.08,.16,.2,.2,.16,.08,.04,.02,.02,.01,.01,0.,0./
 5         DATA REMAL/0.,.0,.,04,.1,.18,.18,.14,.1,.08,.06,.04,.04,.02,.02/
 6         DATA FUND/6*0.,3*.0028,4*.0056,2*.0084,.0112,.014,2*.0168,.014,
 7        *.0112,.0056,.0028/
 8         DATA PAREG/35*0.,20.,9*30.,26.,24.,21.,19.,15.,7.,3./           ***
 9         WRITE(3,240)
10    240 FORMAT(6H1 TIME,6X,7HAPHID I,9X,8HAPHID II,11X,9HAPHID III,14X,
11        *8HAPHID IV,12X,11HAPHID ADULT,10X,8HPARASITE/9X,2(17HWHITE RED GRE ***
12        *EN  ),3(17HWHITE RED   GREEN,5X),12H LARVA MUMMY/              ***
13        *41X,3(13X,9HAPT ALATE)/)                                       ***
14         DO 10 I=1,40
15         ALATE(I)=0.
16         APTRA(I)=0.
17         GYNOP(I)=0.
18         AMALE(I)=0.
19     10 FEM(I)=0.
20         DO 15 I=1,52                                                   ***
21     15 PAR(I)=0.                                                       ***
22         DO 20 I=1,23
23     20 APTRA(I)=FUND(I)
24         GI=APTRA(1)+APTRA(2)+APTRA(3)+APTRA(4)                        ***
25         GII=APTRA(5)+APTRA(6)+APTRA(7)+APTRA(8)                       ***
26         THREE=APTRA(9)+APTRA(10)+APTRA(11)+APTRA(12)
```

```
27          FOUR=APTRA(13)+APTRA(14)+APTRA(15)+APTRA(16)+APTRA(17)+APTRA(18)    ***
28          ADULT=APTRA(19)+APTRA(20)+APTRA(21)+APTRA(22)+APTRA(23)             ***
29          TOT=GI+GII+THREE+FOUR+ADULT                                        ***
30          SR=.61                                                             ***
31          DITOT=0.                                                           ***
32          DO 1000 KF=1,111
33          K=KF-10
34          IF(K-19) 25, 24, 25                                                ***
35       24 PAR(4)=.06                                                         ***
36       25 TN(KF)=TOT                                                         ***
37          A=54.*(1.-K/104.)
38          IF(K) 26, 26, 27
39       26 X=1.
40          GO TO 28
41       27 X=K
42          X=-8.6536+2.959*ALOG(X)-.073*X
43          X=1.-EXP(X)
44       28 REP=A*EXP(-.00096*A*ADULT)*X
45          PGYN=.35*(1.-((K-24.)/30.)**2)
46          IF(PGYN) 30, 40, 40
47       30 PGYN=0.
48       40 PMALE=(1.-PGYN)*(.0105*K-.092)
49          IF(PMALE)50,60,60
50       50 PMALE=0.
51       60 PARTH=1.-PGYN-PMALE
52          PAL=.44-.01*K
53          IF(PAL) 65, 65, 70
54       65 PAL=0.
55       70 EMBRY=0.
56          EM=0.
57          EF=0.
58          DO 100 I=23,36
59          X=ALATE(I+1)+APTRA(I)
60          EMBRY=EMBRY+X*REPAR(I-22)
61          EM=EM+X*REMAL(I-22)
62      100 EF=EF+GYNOP(I+1)*.5*(REMAL(I-22)+REPAR(I-22))
63          EM=EM*PMALE
64          EG=EMBRY*PGYN
65          EA=EMBRY*PARTH
66          I=39
67      140 ALATE(I+1)=ALATE(I)
68          GYNOP(I+1)=GYNOP(I)
69          APTRA(I+1)=APTRA(I)
70          AMALE(I+1)=AMALE(I)
71          FEM(I+1)=FEM(I)
72          I=I-1
73          IF(I) 150, 150, 140
74      150 APTRA(40)=0.
75          FEM(31)=0.
76          AMALE(31)=0.
77          APTRA(1)=EA*REP
78          GYNOP(1)=EG*REP
79          AMALE(1)=EM*REP
80          FEM(1)=EF*REP
81          ALATE(9)=APTRA(9)*PAL
82          APTRA(9)=APTRA(9)-ALATE(9)
83          PARS=.85-.006*K                                                    ***
84          DIAP=.02*(K-67)                                                    ***
85          IF(DIAP) 141, 142, 142                                             ***
86      141 DIAP=0.                                                            ***
87      142 PAREP=0.                                                           ***
88          DO 152 I=36,52                                                     ***
89      152 PAREP=PAREP+PAR(I)*PAREG(I)                                        ***
90          X=THREE+FOUR+APTRA(19)+FEM(19)                                     ***
91          SP=EXP(-PAREP/X)                                                   ***
92          I=51                                                              ***
93      153 PAR(I+1)=PAR(I)                                                    ***
94          I=I-1                                                             ***
95          IF(I) 154, 154, 153                                               ***
96      154 DITOT=DITOT+PAR(35)*DIAP                                           ***
97          PAR(35)=PAR(35)*SR*PARS*(1.-DIAP)                                  ***
98          PAR(1)=X*(1.-SP)                                                   ***
99          PRED=0.
100         IF(K-30) 310, 310, 301
101     301 JS=K-39
102         IF(JS) 302, 302, 303
103     302 JS=1
104     303 JF=K-30
105         DO 304 I=JS,JF
106     304 PRED=PRED+TN(I)
107         PRED=PRED*2.5
108     310 IF(K-20) 320, 320, 311
109     311 JS=K-29
110         IF(JS) 312,312,313
```

```
111        312 JS=1
112        313 JF=K-20
113            DO 314 I=JS,JF
114        314 PRED=PRED+TN(I)
115            PRED=PRED*3.
116        320 IF(K-10) 330, 330, 321
117        321 JS=K-19
118            IF(JS) 322, 322, 323
119        322 JS=1
120        323 JF=K-10
121            DO 324 I=JS,JF
122        324 PRED=PRED+TN(I)
123            PRED=PRED*2.
124        330 IF(K) 340, 340, 331
125        331 JS=K-9
126            IF(JS) 332, 332, 333
127        332 JS=1
128        333 JF=K
129            DO 334 I=JS,JF
130        334 PRED=PRED+TN(I)
131        340 PRED=.00015*PRED
132            SURV=EXP(-PRED/TOT)                                          ***
133            IF(K-35) 180, 180, 155
134        155 ALATE(21)=ALATE(21)*.36
135            GYNOP(21)=GYNOP(21)*.36
136            APTRA(20)=APTRA(20)*.65
137        180 DO 170 I=1,40
138            ALATE(I)=ALATE(I)*SURV
139            GYNOP(I)=GYNOP(I)*SURV
140            AMALE(I)=AMALE(I)*SURV
141            FEM(I)=FEM(I)*SURV
142        170 APTRA(I)=APTRA(I)*SURV
143            DO 172 I=1,22                                                ***
144        172 PAR(I)=PAR(I)*SURV                                          ***
145            DO 175 I=13,19                                              ***
146            ALATE(I)=ALATE(I)*SP                                        ***
147            GYNOP(I)=GYNOP(I)*SP                                        ***
148            AMALE(I)=AMALE(I)*SP                                        ***
149            FEM(I)=FEM(I)*SP                                            ***
150        175 APTRA(I)=APTRA(I)*SP                                        ***
151            GI=0.
152            RI=0.
153            WI=0.
154            GII=0.
155            RII=0.
156            WII=0.
157            GAL3=0.
158            GAP3=0.
159            RIII=0.
160            WIII=0.
161            GAL4=GYNOP(19)+ALATE(19)
162            GAP4=0.
163            RIV=AMALE(19)
164            WIV=0.
165            GALV=0.
166            GAPV=APTRA(19)
167            RV=0.
168            WV=FEM(19)
169            DO 190 I=1,4
170            GI=GI+APTRA(I)+GYNOP(I)
171            RI=RI+AMALE(I)
172        190 WI=WI+FEM(I)
173            DO 191 I=5,8
174            GII=GII+APTRA(I)+GYNOP(I)
175            RII=RII+AMALE(I)
176        191 WII=WII+FEM(I)
177            DO 192 I=9,12
178            GAL3=GAL3+GYNOP(I)+ALATE(I)
179            GAP3=GAP3+APTRA(I)
180            RIII=RIII+AMALE(I)
181        192 WIII=WIII+FEM(I)
182            DO 193 I=13,18
183            GAL4=GAL4+GYNOP(I)+ALATE(I)
184            GAP4=GAP4+APTRA(I)
185            RIV=RIV+AMALE(I)
186        193 WIV=WIV+FEM(I)
187            DO 194 I=20,40
188            GALV=GALV+GYNOP(I)+ALATE(I)
189            GAPV=GAPV+APTRA(I)
190            RV=RV+AMALE(I)
191        194 WV=WV+FEM(I)
192            THREE=GAL3+GAP3+RIII+WIII                                   ***
193            FOUR=GAL4+GAP4+RIV+WIV                                      ***
194            ADULT=GALV+GAPV+RV+WV
```

```
195            TOT=GI+RI+WI+GII+RII+WII+THREE+FOUR+ADULT                          ***
196            IF(K.EQ.7.OR.K.EQ.12.OR.K.EQ.15.OR.K.EQ.20.OR.K.EQ.21)GO TO 200
197            IF(K.EQ.26.OR.K.EQ.30.OR.K.EQ.35.OR.K.EQ.43.OR.K.EQ.52)GO TO 200
198            IF(K.EQ.63.OR.K.EQ.70.OR.K.EQ.81.OR.K.EQ.91)GO TO 200
199            GO TO 1000
200       200  A=13.5*K                                                          ***
201            PARM=0.                                                           ***
202            DO 230 I=24,34                                                    ***
203       230  PARM=PARM+PAR(I)                                                  ***
204            TPAR=0.                                                           ***
205            DO 235 I=7,23                                                     ***
206       235  TPAR=TPAR+PAR(I)                                                  ***
207            WRITE(3,250) A,WI,RI,GI,WII,RII,GII,WIII,RIII,GAP3,GAL3,
208           *WIV,RIV,GAP4,GAL4,WV,RV,GAPV,GALV,TPAR,PARM                       ***
209       250  FORMAT(F6.0,2(2H *,3F5.1),3(2H *,4F5.1),3H **,2F6.2)              ***
210       1000 CONTINUE
211            WRITE(3,260)DITOT                                                 ***
212       260  FORMAT(/27H TOTAL DIAPAUSE PARASITES =,F9.2)                      ***
213            CALL EXIT
214            END
```

OUTPUT FROM VERSION 5

TIME	APHID I WHITE RED GREEN			APHID II WHITE RED GREEN			APHID III WHITE RED GREEN APT ALATE				APHID IV WHITE RED GREEN APT ALATE				APHID ADULT WHITE RED GREEN APT ALATE				PARASI LARVA M
95. *	0.0	0.0	1.3 *	0.0	0.0	2.4 *	0.0	0.0	1.4	1.0 *	0.0	0.0	0.3	0.2 *	0.0	0.0	0.1	0.0 **	0.0
162. *	0.0	0.0	0.4 *	0.0	0.0	1.1 *	0.0	0.0	1.2	0.9 *	0.0	0.0	1.9	1.5 *	0.0	0.0	0.2	0.0 **	0.0
202. *	0.0	0.0	0.1 *	0.0	0.0	0.6 *	0.0	0.0	0.7	0.6 *	0.0	0.0	2.1	1.9 *	0.0	0.0	0.9	0.4 **	0.0
270. *	0.0	0.1	5.0 *	0.0	0.0	0.1 *	0.0	0.0	0.2	0.2 *	0.0	0.0	1.1	1.1 *	0.0	0.0	2.7	1.9 **	0.0
284. *	0.1	0.2	8.8 *	0.0	0.0	0.4 *	0.0	0.0	0.1	0.1 *	0.0	0.0	0.9	1.0 *	0.0	0.0	3.8	2.9 **	0.06
351. *	2.1	2.8	34.2 *	0.2	0.5	13.9 *	0.0	0.0	0.5	0.5 *	0.0	0.0	0.2	0.3 *	0.0	0.0	3.0	2.1 **	0.06
405. *	4.6	4.6	28.3 *	2.1	2.8	34.2 *	0.2	0.5	7.4	6.6 *	0.0	0.0	0.6	0.5 *	0.0	0.0	4.0	3.1 **	0.06
473. *	4.1	3.5	11.2 *	4.8	4.5	24.3 *	2.9	3.5	19.1	16.1 *	0.4	0.9	11.6	10.4 *	0.0	0.0	3.6	3.0 **	0.06
581. *	0.8	0.7	1.9 *	2.3	1.9	3.7 *	4.0	3.4	6.6	4.4 *	6.6	7.3	23.1	22.5 *	1.4	1.5	16.2	8.5 **	0.0
702. *	7.9	8.5	17.7 *	2.8	2.6	11.1 *	0.7	0.6	1.9	0.8 *	3.3	3.4	3.5	2.9 *	10.6	9.9	31.6	14.5 **	0.0
851. *	7.8	12.4	6.2 *	9.8	13.7	10.3 *	9.8	11.9	14.4	0.5 *	7.3	7.6	16.9	3.9 *	4.5	3.4	23.6	10.8 **	3.73
945. *	2.1	4.4	2.6 *	4.9	8.5	3.2 *	7.7	11.8	6.5	0.0 *	13.7	20.2	17.1	0.4 *	9.4	7.2	19.6	4.0 **	6.59
1093. *	1.7	18.1	6.8 *	2.3	11.6	7.0 *	1.5	4.5	4.1	0.0 *	3.7	8.7	2.8	0.0 *	18.3	23.5	21.9	1.2 **	2.32
1228. *	0.0	9.1	1.2 *	0.2	12.7	2.5 *	0.7	13.4	4.0	0.0 *	1.4	9.8	4.7	0.0 *	4.8	8.8	10.7	0.1 **	0.0

TOTAL DIAPAUSE PARASITES =   2.70

quip, laid by adult parasites of age I in the laboratory. Mackauer and van den Bosch (1973) point out that the number of eggs laid may vary with aphid density, but for the present we ignore that complication. The parasites attack third- and fourth-instar, and young adult, aphids. In Table 10.3, THREE and FOUR (lines 26–27) are the total current numbers of third- and fourth-instar aphids. At line 30, SR is the observed proportion of females among the adult parasites which emerged from parasite pupae collected in the field. It did not change with time in any consistent way. DITOT, line 31, accumulates the total number of parasites which enter diapause through the season. The initial rate and timing of parasitization – i.e. the number of eggs laid by the adult parasites which have emerged from winter diapause-were estimated by a special field sample taken at time K = 19. In the model, the parasite population is started by 0·06 parasite larvae (the average number found in the sample) per terminal at time K = 19 (lines 34-35).

When this version of the model was made, we thought that the parasite egg took three quips to hatch, and so we gave the parasite larva an initial age of four: but laboratory work later showed that the true value is more like six quips (Fig. 10.2). PARS, line 83, is the observed rate of survival of parasites from attack by hyperparasites. It was determined by allowing parasites and hyperparasites to emerge individually from samples of parasite pupae collected in the field. DIAP, line 84, is the proportion of pupae currently entering diapause. Diapause mummies are distinguished by their dark colour. PAREP is the total number of eggs which the parasite females are trying to lay during the current time-step. It is calculated from the numbers of adult parasites of various ages (PAR) and their appropriate fecundities (lines 87-89). Line 91 calculates the proportion SP of instar III, IV and early adult aphids which escape parasitization, using the Thompson exponential formula of Chapter 4. In line 97, the proportions SR, PARS and DIAP are all applied to the parasites when they first emerge as adults, at age 35 quips. Therefore, PAR(I) represents the total number of all parasites of age I, when I < 35, but only the adult female parasites thereafter. The maturing diapause parasites are added into the running total, DITOT, at line 96. Line 131 readjusts the syrphid egg-laying rate to give the correct (observed) numbers of syrphid larvae. The syrphids will willingly eat parasitized aphids aged 1-22 quips, which are therefore included in the number of aphids at risk (lines 143-144): and the numbers of all aphids aged 13-19 are adjusted for losses due to parasitization (lines 145-150).

Here we admit a mistake: it is, in fact, the aphids aged 9-19, and not 13-19, which are liable to parasitization. This mistake, which has gone undetected for several years, does not make much difference to the numerical answers, since the correct numbers of new parasites are computed at line 98: we have left it unchanged, just to show how carefully the model should be checked!

The numerical output at the end of Table 10.3 gives far too few first-generation parasites, and the parasite generations are much too discrete. The special sample used to estimate the initial rate of parasitization was evidently a failure. It was taken at time K = 19 quips or 260 day-$^\circ$F, when the first generation of parasites had hardly begun (Table 10.5). Table 10.4 therefore substitutes a table PARIM of first-generation parasite eggs, chosen purely empirically to give the right

Table 10.4

```
1   C       PROGRAM MASONAPHIS - APHIDIUS (SIXTH VERSION)
2           DIMENSION ALATE(40),APTRA(40),GYNOP(40),AMALE(40),FEM(40),
3          *REPAR(14),REMAL(14),FUND(23),TN(120),PAR(52),PAREG(52),PARIM(30)    ***
4           DATA REPAR/.02,.08,.16,.2,.2,.16,.08,.04,.02,.02,.01,.01,0.,0./
5           DATA REMAL/0.,0.,.04,.1,.18,.18,.14,.1,.08,.06,.04,.04,.02,.02/
6           DATA FUND/6*0.,3*.0028,4*.0056,2*.0084,.0112,.014,2*.0168,.014,
7          *.0112,.0056,.0028/
8           DATA PAREG/35*0.,20.,9*30.,26.,24.,21.,19.,15.,7.,3./
9           DATA PARIM/5*0.,.01,.03,.04,.04,4*.03,6*.02,4*.01,7*0./            ***
10          P=.7                                                               ***
11          Q=1.                                                               ***
12          DO 5 I=37,52                                                       ***
13          Q=Q*P                                                             ***
14        5 PAREG(I)=PAREG(I)*Q                                               ***
15          WRITE(3,240)
16      240 FORMAT(6H1 TIME,6X,7HAPHID I,9X,8HAPHID II,11X,9HAPHID III,14X,
17         *8HAPHID IV,12X,11HAPHID ADULT,10X,8HPARASITE/9X,2(17HWHITE RED GRE
18         *EN ),3(17HWHITE RED   GREEN,5X),12H LARVA MUMMY/
19         *41X,3(13X,9HAPT ALATE)/)
20          DO 10 I=1,40
21          ALATE(I)=0.
22          APTRA(I)=0.
23          GYNOP(I)=0.
24          AMALE(I)=0.
25       10 FEM(I)=0.
26          DO 15 I=1,52
27       15 PAR(I)=0.
28          DO 20 I=1,23
29       20 APTRA(I)=FUND(I)
30          GI=APTRA(1)+APTRA(2)+APTRA(3)+APTRA(4)
31          GII=APTRA(5)+APTRA(6)+APTRA(7)+APTRA(8)
32          THREE=APTRA(9)+APTRA(10)+APTRA(11)+APTRA(12)
33          FOUR=APTRA(13)+APTRA(14)+APTRA(15)+APTRA(16)+APTRA(17)+APTRA(18)
34          ADULT=APTRA(19)+APTRA(20)+APTRA(21)+APTRA(22)+APTRA(23)
35          TOT=GI+GII+THREE+FOUR+ADULT
36          SR=.61
37          DITOT=0.
38          TFEM=0.                                                           ***
39          DO 1000 KF=1,114                                                  ***
40          K=KF-10
41          IF(K-1) 25, 21, 21                                                ***
42       21 IF(K-30) 22, 22, 25                                               ***
43       22 PAR(1)=PARIM(K)                                                   ***
44       25 TN(KF)=TOT
45          A=54.*(1.-K/104.)
46          IF(A) 700, 710, 710                                              ***
47      700 A=0.                                                              ***
48      710 IF(K) 26, 26, 27                                                  ***
49       26 X=1.
50          GO TO 28
51       27 X=K
52          X=-8.6536+2.959*ALOG(X)-.073*X
53          X=1.-EXP(X)
```

```
54      28 REP=A*EXP(-.00096*A*ADULT)*X
55         IF(K-40) 31, 31, 32                                    ***
56      31 PGYN=.01*(K+11)
57         GO TO 40                                               ***
58      32 PGYN=.02*(65-K)
59         IF(PGYN) 30, 40, 40
60      30 PGYN=0.
61      40 PMALE=(1.-PGYN)*(.0105*K-.092)
62         IF(PMALE) 50, 55, 55                                   ***
63      50 PMALE=0.
64         GO TO 60                                               ***
65      55 IF(PMALE-1.) 60, 60, 56                                ***
66      56 PMALE=1.                                               ***
67      60 PARTH=1.-PGYN-PMALE
68         PAL=.44-.01*K
69         IF(PAL) 65, 65, 70
70      65 PAL=0.
71      70 EMBRY=0.
72         EM=0.
73         EF=0.
74         DO 100 I=23,36
75         X=ALATE(I+1)+APTRA(I)
76         EMBRY=EMBRY+X*REPAR(I-22)
77         EM=EM+X*REMAL(I-22)
78     100 EF=EF+GYNOP(I+1)*.5*(REMAL(I-22)+REPAR(I-22))
79         EM=EM*PMALE
80         EG=EMBRY*PGYN
81         EA=EMBRY*PARTH
82         I=39
83     140 ALATE(I+1)=ALATE(I)
84         GYNOP(I+1)=GYNOP(I)
85         APTRA(I+1)=APTRA(I)
86         AMALE(I+1)=AMALE(I)
87         FEM(I+1)=FEM(I)
88         I=I-1
89         IF(I) 150, 150, 140
90     150 APTRA(40)=0.
91         FEM(31)=0.
92         AMALE(31)=0.
93         APTRA(1)=EA*REP
94         GYNOP(1)=EG*REP
95         AMALE(1)=EM*REP
96         FEM(1)=EF*REP
97         ALATE(9)=APTRA(9)*PAL
98         APTRA(9)=APTRA(9)-ALATE(9)
99         PARS=.85-.006*K
100        DIAP=.01*(K-17)                                        ***
101        IF(DIAP) 141, 142, 142
102    141 DIAP=0.
103    142 PAREP=0.
104        DO 152 I=36,52
105    152 PAREP=PAREP+PAR(I)*PAREG(I)
106        X=THREE+FOUR+APTRA(19)+FEM(19)
107        Y=X                                                    ***
108        DO 145 I=1,6                                           ***
109    145 Y=Y+PAR(I)                                             ***
110        SP=EXP(-PAREP/Y)                                       ***
111        I=51
112    153 PAR(I+1)=PAR(I)
113        I=I-1
114        IF(I) 154, 154, 153
115    154 DITOT=DITOT+PAR(35)*DIAP*SR*PARS                       ***
116        PAR(35)=PAR(35)*SR*PARS*(1.-DIAP)
117        PAR(1)=X*(1.-SP)
118        PRED=0.
119        IF(K-30) 310, 310, 301
120    301 JS=K-39
121        IF(JS) 302, 302, 303
122    302 JS=1
123    303 JF=K-30
124        DO 304 I=JS,JF
125    304 PRED=PRED+TN(I)
126        PRED=PRED*2.5
127    310 IF(K-20) 320, 320, 311
128    311 JS=K-29
129        IF(JS) 312,312,313
130    312 JS=1
131    313 JF=K-20
132        DO 314 I=JS,JF
133    314 PRED=PRED+TN(I)
134        PRED=PRED*3.
135    320 IF(K-10) 330, 330, 321
136    321 JS=K-19
137        IF(JS) 322, 322, 323
```

127

```
138      322 JS=1
139      323 JF=K-10
140          DO 324 I=JS,JF
141      324 PRED=PRED+TN(I)
142          PRED=PRED*2.
143      330 IF(K) 340, 340, 331
144      331 JS=K-9
145          IF(JS) 332, 332, 333
146      332 JS=1
147      333 JF=K
148          DO 334 I=JS,JF
149      334 PRED=PRED+TN(I)
150      340 PRED=.00015*PRED
151          SURV=EXP(-PRED/TOT)
152          IF(K-35) 180, 180, 155
153      155 ALATE(21)=ALATE(21)*.36
154          GYNOP(21)=GYNOP(21)*.36
155          APTRA(20)=APTRA(20)*.65
156      180 DO 170 I=1,40
157          ALATE(I)=ALATE(I)*SURV
158          GYNOP(I)=GYNOP(I)*SURV
159          AMALE(I)=AMALE(I)*SURV
160          FEM(I)=FEM(I)*SURV
161      170 APTRA(I)=APTRA(I)*SURV                                    ***
162          TOT=0.
163          DO 172 I=1,22                                             ***
164          PAR(I)=PAR(I)*SURV                                        ***
165      172 TOT=TOT+PAR(I)
166          DO 175 I=13,19
167          ALATE(I)=ALATE(I)*SP
168          GYNOP(I)=GYNOP(I)*SP
169          AMALE(I)=AMALE(I)*SP
170          FEM(I)=FEM(I)*SP
171      175 APTRA(I)=APTRA(I)*SP
172          TFEM=TFEM+FEM(19)                                         ***
173          GI=0.
174          RI=0.
175          WI=0.
176          GII=0.
177          RII=0.
178          WII=0.
179          GAL3=0.
180          GAP3=0.
181          RIII=0.
182          WIII=0.
183          GAL4=GYNOP(19)+ALATE(19)
184          GAP4=0.
185          RIV=AMALE(19)
186          WIV=0.
187          GALV=0.
188          GAPV=APTRA(19)
189          RV=0.
190          WV=FEM(19)
191          DO 190 I=1,4
192          GI=GI+APTRA(I)+GYNOP(I)
193          RI=RI+AMALE(I)
194      190 WI=WI+FEM(I)
195          DO 191 I=5,8
196          GII=GII+APTRA(I)+GYNOP(I)
197          RII=RII+AMALE(I)
198      191 WII=WII+FEM(I)
199          DO 192 I=9,12
200          GAL3=GAL3+GYNOP(I)+ALATE(I)
201          GAP3=GAP3+APTRA(I)
202          RIII=RIII+AMALE(I)
203      192 WIII=WIII+FEM(I)
204          DO 193 I=13,18
205          GAL4=GAL4+GYNOP(I)+ALATE(I)
206          GAP4=GAP4+APTRA(I)
207          RIV=RIV+AMALE(I)
208      193 WIV=WIV+FEM(I)
209          DO 194 I=20,40
210          GALV=GALV+GYNOP(I)+ALATE(I)
211          GAPV=GAPV+APTRA(I)
212          RV=RV+AMALE(I)
213      194 WV=WV+FEM(I)
214          THREE=GAL3+GAP3+RIII+WIII
215          FOUR=GAL4+GAP4+RIV+WIV
216          ADULT=GALV+GAPV+RV+WV
217          TOT=TOT+GI+RI+WI+GII+RII+WII+THREE+FOUR+ADULT            ***
218          IF(K.EQ.7.OR.K.EQ.12.OR.K.EQ.15.OR.K.EQ.20.OR.K.EQ.21)GO TO 200
219          IF(K.EQ.26.OR.K.EQ.30.OR.K.EQ.35.OR.K.EQ.43.OR.K.EQ.52)GO TO 200
220          IF(K.EQ.63.OR.K.EQ.70.OR.K.EQ.81.OR.K.EQ.91)GO TO 200
221          GO TO 1000
```

```
222    200 A=13.5*K
223        PARM=0.
224        DO 230 I=24,34
225    230 PARM=PARM+PAR(I)
226        TPAR=0.
227        DO 235 I=7,23
228    235 TPAR=TPAR+PAR(I)
229        WRITE(3,250) A,WI,RI,GI,WII,RII,GII,WIII,RIII,GAP3,GAL3,
230       *WIV,RIV,GAP4,GAL4,WV,RV,GAPV,GALV,TPAR,PARM
231    250 FORMAT(F6.0,2(2H *,3F5.1),3(2H *,4F5.1),3H **,2F6.2)
232   1000 CONTINUE
233        WRITE(3,260)TFEM,DITOT                                    ***
234    260 FORMAT(/23H TOTAL APHID OVIPARAE =,F9.1,                  ***
235       *42H  TOTAL VIABLE FEMALE DIAPAUSE PARASITES =,F9.2)       ***
236        CALL EXIT
237        END
```

OUTPUT FROM VERSION 6

ME	APHID I WHITE RED GREEN	APHID II WHITE RED GREEN	APHID III WHITE RED GREEN APT ALATE	APHID IV WHITE RED GREEN APT ALATE	APHID ADULT WHITE RED GREEN APT ALATE	PARASITE LARVA MUMMY
*	0.0 0.0 1.3 *	0.0 0.0 2.4 *	0.0 0.0 1.4 1.1 *	0.0 0.0 0.3 0.2 *	0.0 0.0 0.1 0.0 **	0.0 0.0
*	0.0 0.0 0.4 *	0.0 0.0 1.1 *	0.0 0.0 1.2 0.9 *	0.0 0.0 1.9 1.6 *	0.0 0.0 0.2 0.0 **	0.04 0.0
*	0.0 0.0 0.1 *	0.0 0.0 0.6 *	0.0 0.0 0.8 0.6 *	0.0 0.0 2.2 1.9 *	0.0 0.0 0.9 0.4 **	0.15 0.0
*	0.1 0.1 4.7 *	0.0 0.0 0.1 *	0.0 0.0 0.2 0.2 *	0.0 0.0 1.1 1.1 *	0.0 0.0 2.7 1.9 **	0.28 0.0
*	0.2 0.2 8.5 *	0.0 0.0 0.4 *	0.0 0.0 0.2 0.1 *	0.0 0.0 1.0 0.9 *	0.0 0.0 3.0 2.1 **	0.30 0.0
*	2.5 2.7 34.1 *	0.4 0.5 13.5 *	0.0 0.0 0.5 0.4 *	0.0 0.0 0.3 0.3 *	0.0 0.0 3.9 2.8 **	0.38 0.0
*	4.1 4.2 29.4 *	2.5 2.7 34.1 *	0.4 0.5 7.4 6.0 *	0.0 0.0 0.6 0.5 *	0.0 0.0 4.1 3.1 **	0.32 0.08
*	3.2 2.9 12.4 *	4.1 4.2 25.5 *	3.1 3.3 18.7 16.8 *	0.8 0.9 11.7 9.7 *	0.0 0.0 3.8 2.9 **	0.16 0.24
*	0.6 0.5 2.2 *	1.8 1.4 4.3 *	3.2 2.9 5.7 6.5 *	5.9 6.8 21.7 25.1 *	2.0 1.5 16.2 8.1 **	0.02 0.23
*	8.1 6.9 21.3 *	2.5 2.0 12.8 *	0.6 0.4 1.4 1.7 *	2.4 2.6 2.7 4.8 *	9.3 8.8 29.6 15.5 **	2.52 0.04
*	10.7 10.6 6.0 *	12.3 11.8 11.7 *	11.1 10.0 11.7 6.7 *	7.2 6.2 13.7 12.2 *	3.6 2.7 21.0 12.9 **	6.79 0.0
*	3.9 3.6 2.1 *	7.4 7.2 2.8 *	10.4 10.2 5.4 1.2 *	16.5 17.3 14.1 8.5 *	9.5 6.0 16.0 8.9 **	4.15 2.87
*	7.7 14.7 5.5 *	6.6 9.4 5.7 *	3.5 3.7 3.3 0.0 *	5.1 6.2 1.9 0.1 *	22.8 20.2 18.1 6.0 **	0.36 3.46
*	1.4 7.6 0.9 *	3.3 11.1 2.2 *	5.0 11.4 3.4 0.0 *	6.4 10.7 5.2 0.0 *	6.3 5.6 8.6 1.9 **	11.30 0.49

AL APHID OVIPARAE =   60.3 TOTAL VIABLE FEMALE DIAPAUSE PARASITES =   0.97

numbers and timing for the first parasite generation. The second generation of parasites then becomes far too large. If the adult parasites all emerged successfully, and laid all their eggs, the numbers of parasites would build up far more rapidly than they actually do. So Table 10.4 introduces a per-quip survival rate P for adult parasites. Strictly speaking, that survival-rate should be applied to the numbers of adult parasites in each age-interval at each time-step. But the end result is the same, at considerable saving in computer time, if the survival rate P is applied instead to the numbers of eggs laid by adults of successive ages, as in lines 9–14. The value of P is chosen purely empirically to give the right ratio of 2nd : 1st generation parasites. It reduces the average parasite fecundity from the 405 observed in the laboratory to 89. Obviously, a lot is still unknown about the parasites – why the adults have poor survival and whether 'random search' accurately predicts the parasitization rate.

Aphid-parasite and aphid-predator relationships

Table 10.4 makes several other small changes to the program. It changes the values of a few parameters to make them more realistic: the changes, all fairly small, are made empirically to diminish discrepancies between observation and prediction, but only when the discrepancy is clearly due to one particular parameter. Table 10.4 recognizes that aphids which contain parasite eggs may be parasitized again (lines 107–110). This is not true of aphids which contain parasite larvae. Since only one parasite eventually emerges from an aphid containing several parasite eggs, there is no need to alter the formulae which specify how many adult parasites shall emerge. DITOT now accumulates the total number of viable female diapause parasites only (line 115). It is an underestimate, because it ignores all immature parasite pupae, aged less than 35 quips, remaining at the end of the season. We do not know how many such pupae would survive: the omission is not serious, because most pupae are lost to hyperparasitism at the end of the season. The program accumulates a new running total, TFEM, of aphid oviparae through the season. So DITOT is the number of female parasites which enter winter diapause, and TFEM is proportional to the number of overwintering aphid eggs. Those two totals, which record the 'fitness' of parasite and aphid respectively through the season, are needed for the test described in Chapter 3. Neither can be observed directly: they can be estimated only from the model itself.

We think that the output of Table 10.4 reproduces the original field data well enough. The agreement between prediction and observation in Table 10.4 is more obvious when the same numbers are drawn as histograms in Fig. 10.3. The agreement could no doubt be improved by various fine adjustments, but there is no biological reason why we should do so. It is clear that, whereas the aphid life-table is largely based on ascertained biological facts, the representation of the parasite is much more conjectural. It is therefore no surprise to find that the aphid passes the test of Chapter 3, but the parasite does not (Gilbert and Gutierrez 1973). Simulation model or no simulation model, this discussion has brought to light the numerous pieces of information which *must* be specified if we are to describe and understand the ecological relationships. It is unlikely that any ecologist could write down, off-hand, the entire list of the pieces of information which have proved to be necessary (whether or not we actually collected them!). That such models do indeed oblige us to recognize, and to specify explicitly, the vital pieces of information is perhaps their greatest merit, at present.

Aphid-parasite and aphid-predator relationships

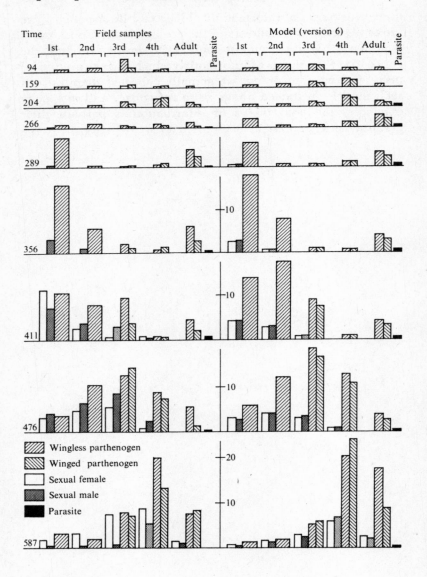

Aphid-parasite and aphid-predator relationships

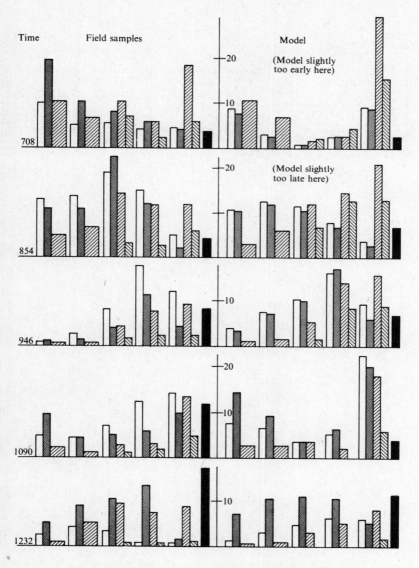

Fig. 10.3 Comparison of *Masonaphis* model and field samples.

Aphid-parasite and aphid-predator relationships

Table 10.5

TIME	APHID I WHITE	RED	GREEN	APHID II WHITE	RED	GREEN	FIELD DATA APHID III WHITE	RED	GREEN APT	ALATE	APHID IV WHITE	RED	GREEN APT	ALATE	APHID ADULT WHITE	RED	GREEN APT	ALATE	PARAS LARVA
94.	0.0	0.0	1.1	0.0	0.0	1.4	0.0	0.0	3.0	0.9	0.0	0.0	0.1	0.5	0.0	0.0	0.1	0.0	0.0
159.	0.0	0.0	0.3	0.0	0.0	1.2	0.0	0.0	0.9	1.0	0.0	0.0	0.3	0.4	0.0	0.0	0.1	0.0	0.0
204.	0.0	0.0	0.4	0.0	0.0	0.8	0.0	0.0	1.3	0.9	0.0	0.0	1.9	2.2	0.0	0.0	1.0	0.1	0.0
266.	0.0	0.1	1.7	0.0	0.0	2.6	0.0	0.0	0.6	0.2	0.0	0.0	0.9	0.5	0.0	0.0	1.3	0.3	0.05
289.	0.0	0.6	13.4	0.0	0.0	0.6	0.0	0.0	0.2	0.3	0.0	0.0	0.5	1.0	0.0	0.0	4.0	2.4	0.03
356.	0.0	3.4	30.7	0.0	1.2	11.4	0.0	0.0	2.2	1.2	0.0	0.0	0.7	1.5	0.0	0.0	6.1	2.8	0.40
411.	11.3	7.1	21.9	2.7	3.8	15.8	0.7	2.8	9.4	3.7	0.7	0.2	0.9	0.8	0.0	0.0	4.4	2.0	0.38
476.	3.2	4.2	7.4	4.9	6.6	21.3	5.8	8.7	12.6	14.2	0.8	2.3	8.9	7.5	0.0	0.0	5.7	1.4	0.29
587.	2.0	0.3	7.1	3.2	0.2	4.1	7.6	0.8	8.0	7.0	8.9	5.3	20.0	13.2	1.5	1.0	7.7	8.2	0.0
708.	10.1	19.5	20.6	5.0	10.3	13.1	5.3	8.1	10.3	7.0	4.0	5.6	5.6	2.0	4.3	4.0	18.3	5.9	2.58
854.	12.9	10.9	9.7	13.5	10.9	13.0	18.9	22.4	14.0	2.9	14.7	11.9	11.6	2.3	4.8	1.7	11.5	5.6	3.77
946.	0.7	1.0	0.9	2.5	1.3	1.1	8.2	4.0	4.2	1.6	18.0	11.3	7.9	2.1	12.1	4.2	9.3	2.2	6.23
1090.	4.9	9.7	4.4	4.5	4.6	2.1	7.1	5.0	2.8	1.0	12.4	5.8	3.0	1.9	14.4	9.9	13.5	4.8	4.70
1232.	2.5	5.3	1.9	4.5	9.2	11.0	3.7	10.9	9.7	0.6	0.9	13.7	7.6	0.7	0.8	1.8	9.0	1.0	12.62

11 PARTICULAR TYPES OF RELATIONSHIP

Chapters 9 and 10 described, in some detail, the construction of a general population model. Here we shall briefly survey the technical pecularities of the different kinds of ecological relationship mentioned in Chapters 4-6. For fuller details, the reader should consult the detailed descriptions available on request from the authors of the original papers.

Predator-prey relationship

As stated in Chapter 4, the detailed study of predation in the field involves observation of the predation process itself, i.e. of the behaviour of individual predators and prey; and translation of the results into a mathematical expression that will predict the predation rate in all circumstances encountered in the field. (But where the predator has no serious impact on prey numbers, i.e. where the density-dependent mechanisms which affect the prey numbers can easily make good the losses to predation, simplistic theoretical expressions for predation rate may be good enough.) The dominant variable in the description of the predation process is physiological time, because that is the primary variable which restricts the predator's success. 'Restricted time' therefore replaces the conventional notion of a limited 'area of search'.

In the coccinellid case of Chapter 4, the predator searches one plant after another. Each successive plant is chosen at random; there is no evidence that the coccinellid tends to move in any fixed direction up or down the row, and it often searches the same plant several times. Nor does it choose plants bearing many aphids in preference to those with few or none. If the predator searched more methodically, the model would have to be amended accordingly. The predator cannot detect the aphids at any distance; it finds them solely by running into them. An aphid may escape by falling off the plant when it feels the predator advancing towards it. If the aphid falls off a plant, it climbs on to a new plant chosen at random, i.e. without reference to the number of aphids already on that plant. Old aphids fall off more readily than young, presumably because they have less trouble finding a new plant. When the predator searches a plant, therefore, each aphid on the plant has a fixed probability of leaving the plant; but that probability varies according to the aphid's age. The predator has a certain probability of contacting each remaining aphid. That probability increases with the predator's hunger (defined as the biomass of aphid which the predator will currently eat to satiation), because hungry coccinellids search more anxiously than less hungry individuals. Once the predator has contacted an aphid, it has a fixed probability of capturing it; that probability again varies according to the age of the aphid, because older aphids can escape from the predator's grasp more easily than can young ones. When the predator eats an aphid, its hunger is reduced according to the biomass of the aphid. If the predator searches a plant without contacting any aphids, it spends a fixed average time on that plant, and its hunger increases accordingly. If it contacts an aphid but does not capture it, it searches the plant more thoroughly, and therefore spends a longer average time on the plant. The probability of contacting further aphids is consequently increased. If the coccinellid captures one or more aphids, the total time spent on the plant is increased by the time taken to eat the prey, which is proportional to the biomass of the prey.

These simple rules are built into a simulation model of the predation process, which predicts the numbers of aphids eaten, given the initial numbers and age-distribution of prey present on the plants. Except for the equation which describes how the predator's hunger increases with time, all the equations in the model are linear. When the total time spent searching has reached one quip, the computer prints the number and ages of aphids eaten. Whenever there is a specified probability of some event (e.g. capture of an aphid), the model compares that probability with a freshly-chosen random number, and accordingly decides whether or not the event shall occur. By using different sets of random numbers, therefore, the model gives different answers, and so generates a whole set of possible outcomes, from which the predation rate – i.e. the *frequency* of predation per quip – is estimated. This use of repeated trials to determine a frequency is known as the 'Monte Carlo' method.

The method of describing the predation process is identical to that used by Holling (1966), except for the necessary changes in the biological details. The technical difficulty lies not in making the model itself, but in estimating the various parameters in the field, and especially in deciding what are the important biological variables. For example, the preliminary model of predation in the laboratory included three more variables, *viz.* the size of each plant, the distribution of numbers of aphids per plant (not just the average number) and the time elapsed since the coccinellid last contacted an aphid (as well as the coccinellid's hunger). We found that these three variables could be omitted from the study of predation in the field, and consequently the 'contact' mechanism could be eliminated altogether, i.e. the rules for 'contact' could be combined with those for 'capture'. But those three variables, or still others, may well prove to be important for other predators and other prey. A subsequent technical difficulty lies in the translation from the level of individual behaviour to the level of population dynamics (Chapter 4), i.e. in fitting a mathematical expression to predict the predation rate in all circumstances which might be encountered in the field. But this is purely a problem in applied mathematics and therefore need not be discussed here.

Plant–herbivore relationship

The main point here is that a population of plants, or rather of parts (roots, leaves etc.) of plants, may be analysed in much the same way that populations of animals were analysed in Chapters 9 and 10. As an example, we choose the work of

Particular types of relationship

Gutierrez, Falcon *et al.* (1975) on cotton.

For reasons stated in Chapter 5, this work describes the development and growth, not of a single cotton plant, but of all the plants on a unit area of land. The basic principle is that of a carbohydrate pool. Carbohydrate is added to the pool by photosynthesis and is used partly to maintain the plant's metabolism and partly to grow new tissues. Since in this case the plants are well fertilized and watered, their growth is limited by the rate of photosynthesis. Where that is not the case, it is easy enough to add restrictions due to shortage of water, nitrogen, or other elements, once the plant physiology is understood (McArthur *et al.* 1975). The input to the carbohydrate pool is measured in terms of photosynthate production, but the drain on the pool is measured in terms of the increase in dry matter of the various parts of the plant. The plant's uptake of dry matter through the roots is therefore assumed to be negligible, as indeed it is on a weight-for-weight basis.

Since photosynthesis is a daily event, it has proved most convenient to use one day as the basic time-step for the simulation model. Each day's maximum and minimum temperatures then give the corresponding increments of physiological time, both for the plants and for the insects which attack the plants. The plants and insects have sharply different temperature thresholds for development, and therefore operate on different physiological time-scales. The day's production of photosynthate is calculated as a function of insolation, temperature, leaf mass etc. The formula for photosynthate production is an empirical regression equation developed by Hesketh *et al.* (1971). Although derived elsewhere for different varieties of cotton, the formula works well for the Acala variety of cotton grown in California. But the rules for dividing up the carbohydrate supply among the various parts of the plants were worked out to suit the Californian field data. These rules are:

(a) *Priority of distribution*. The available carbohydrate is used, first, to meet the daily respiratory demand for maintenance of the existing plant tissues: then to develop the fruit, if any are present on the plant: and then the remaining carbohydrate, if any, is shared out *pro rata* to initiate new stems, roots and leaves in proportion to their respective demands. Excess carbohydrate is stored for future use.

(*b*) *Growth*. Each piece of plant tissue is initiated, grows for a fixed period of physiological time and then matures. Each plant part (root, leaf etc.) has a different maturation time. Therefore, each plant part is divided into a series of age-classes, just as the aphids and parasites in Chapters 9 and 10 were divided into age-classes. Since the plant model works in terms of dry weight, the computer records not the numbers, but the total weights, in each age-class. In all other respects, the plant and aphid models work in the same way: each age-class is moved up into the next class at the appropriate intervals of physiological time, each age-class experiences the appropriate survival-rate and the lowest age-class is filled by reproduction or by initiation of new plant tissue. The rate of photosynthesis itself depends on the age-structure of the leaves, because photosynthetic efficiency declines as the leaf ages.

(*c*) *Initiation*. Main stems of the plants are initiated at a rate which increases linearly with physiological time, i.e. as the season progresses, but which is diminished by effects of plant crowding (expressed in terms of planting density), and may be temporarily decreased, as described above in (*a*), if there is not enough carbohydrate to go round. Roots and leaves follow similar rules, except that their rates of initiation increase exponentially as the season progresses and the plants grow bigger. The rules for fruit are similar, except that there is a time-delay before each mainstem begins to produce fruiting branches, and young fruit below a certain age may be shed if there is not enough carbohydrate to support their development. For comparison with the field data, the model records numbers of fruit, as well as their biomass.

These rules, built into a simulation model, give an excellent description of the actual growth of the plants under varying conditions. The model is obviously very similar in principle to the aphid model of Chapter 9. Initiation rates correspond to birth-rates, plant parts to aphid morphs, and age-groups to age-groups. The effects of insect attack on the cotton are then added in much the same way that the effects of predators and parasites were added in Chapter 10. One species of insect attacks plant leaves of a particular age-range, while another species attacks fruit of another age-range. The effects on the plant are represented by the appropriate survival-rates applied to the appropriate categories in the plant model. Where the insects are polyphagous, their numbers must be taken for granted: but where they are restricted to the one host plant, at least locally, their reproductive rate is determined by the biomass which they capture from the plants, and so their numbers may in turn be represented in the model by a life-table with birth-rates expressed as the appropriate function of plant damage (Chapter 5). In that case, the complete insect–plant relationship can be built into the model, just as a complete parasite–aphid relationship could be described in Chapter 10. Therefore, the methods of analysis of plant–herbivore and predator–prey relationships are in principle the same, however different the biological details may be.

Animal movement

Here we return to the level of individual behaviour. For it is not enough, when studying animal movement, merely to record the distribution of animals after some fixed interval of time (Chapter 6). To predict how the animals will move in all the circumstances which they may encounter in the field, we must necessarily study the process of movement itself. The only cases where the process has been studied in detail, and linked to the subsequent effects on the population dynamics, are those of the caterpillar and butterfly mentioned in Chapter 6. Here we shall briefly discuss the butterfly case, which describes the flight and egglaying behaviour of *Pieris rapae* females. Since the butterflies move and lay their eggs independently of each other, any given density of butterflies may be represented simply by superimposing the results for the appropriate number of individuals. So the simulation model predicts the distribution of eggs over any given arrangement of plants, for any density of butterflies.

For convenience of computation, the area is divided into a square Cartesian grid, the distance from one point to the next being one metre. Every point on the grid contains either a host plant of known species and age, a flower, or simply 'grass' on which the butterfly may land, but on which she cannot feed or lay eggs. The butterfly moves over this grid in a series of unit steps, according to specified rules. Her movement is technically a 'directed random walk', complicated by attraction to host plants. No time-scale is involved. The rules of movement were deduced by watching butterflies fly from point to point over experimental arrangements of host plants, recording their movements and checking each host plant visited for eggs.

From any point on the grid, the butterfly may take a unit step in any of eight directions (Fig. 11.1). The butterfly has a preferred direction of flight, i.e. a tendency to move in one

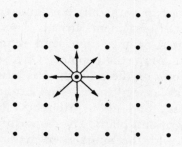

Fig. 11.1 Permitted unit steps in butterfly flight model.

particular direction. Different individuals have different preferred directions. She also has a tendency to move in the same direction as in the previous step, whether or not that previous step was in her preferred direction. And she is attracted to host plants, i.e. she is more likely to move to a given point on the grid if it contains a host plant than if it does not. The simulation model combines these rules to calculate, at each successive step, the probabilities of movement in each of the eight possible directions. The model then selects a random number and compares it with the eight probabilities, in order to decide in which direction the butterfly shall actually move. Like the description of individual predator behaviour, therefore, this description of individual butterfly behaviour is stochastic and is analysed by the 'Monte Carlo' method.

Having taken a unit step, the butterfly does not necessarily alight. There is a further probability, to decide whether she shall land at each new point on the grid. The butterflies may therefore travel some considerable distance before landing. A butterfly is more likely to land on a host plant or on a flower than on 'grass'; so the probability of landing varies accordingly. Having landed on a host plant, the butterflies often hop to different parts of the plant before leaving it, and so may lay several eggs in succession on the same plant. The model therefore includes a further probability that the butterfly shall not move at all, but land again at the same point. The rules of movement, already described, also permit her to move away from a plant and return to it, without landing at any intermediate point. Once the butterfly has landed at any point on the grid, there is a further probability that she shall lay an egg there. That probability is zero for 'flower' or 'grass', and takes different values for different species and ages of host plant. The degree of attraction to host plants increases with the numbers of mature eggs which the butterfly has to lay. In other words, butterflies with few eggs left to lay become more exacting in their choice of host plant.

That these simple rules predict very well the patterns of eggs laid has been confirmed both by observation and experiment

(Chapter 7). The use of a grid, although convenient, is not essential: in the simpler case of caterpillars searching for new host plants, no grid is used and the animals may travel in any direction on a horizontal plane. A hungry caterpillar is observed to move in much straighter lines, and much faster, than a replete one. The simulation model for caterpillar movement therefore includes a physiological time-scale and a hunger mechanism. Thus the form – not just the parameters – of the model is chosen in accordance with biological reality.

To sum up, then, the dynamics of animal populations, and the relationships between them, can often be understood only when the behaviour of the individual animals has been studied. We generally use stochastic simulation models of individual behaviour and deterministic 'variable life-table' models for population interactions. The simulation model has no intrinsic value: it merely synthesizes our biological knowledge, or ignorance. Broadly similar methods are used for quite different biological problems, but the details must always correspond to biological reality. There may be some technical difficulty in translating the numerical results of individual behaviour into the birth- and survival-rates used in a population model; but the main technical problem at present is to devise and implement methods for estimating the relevant biological components in the field.

APPENDIX

A note on theories of scientific inference, and their implications for ecological research

In Chapter 1 we argued that field studies are the key to any understanding of ecology. Some readers have protested that our argument disregards current ideas on the nature of scientific research. This appendix therefore surveys, very superficially, the problem of scientific inference. That problem is unsolved, and so the following treatment is certainly not definitive. Perhaps we lesser mortals should not bother our heads over a problem that has defeated (among others) Bertrand Russell, J. M. Keynes, R. A. Fisher and Sir Harold Jeffreys. For it is true that few scientists rigorously follow the 'rules' of scientific research in their daily work. But perhaps ecologists would be more successful if they obeyed stringent rules for formulating, testing and negating theoretical hypotheses?

The problem of inference is best posed as an example. As long as anyone can remember, the sun has always risen every morning. What reason have we to believe – as we surely do – that the sun will also rise tomorrow? On what logical basis can we infer that, because some event has occurred regularly in the past, it will continue to do so in the future? Any possible argument must necessarily rely on evidence which has been collected only in the past, and which therefore tells us nothing *directly* about future events. (To say that if the sun didn't rise tomorrow, it wouldn't *be* tomorrow, merely evades the logical problem!) Yet the whole of science, and most of everyday life, depends on countless inferences from past experience to future events.

The problem, then, is to find logical rules that will justify the very process of inference itself and that will distinguish valid inferences from false ones. This problem is attacked by philosophers and by statisticians. As might be expected, there are diverse schools of thought within each field, but the philosophers usually ignore the efforts of the statisticians, and vice versa. Yet the arguments are very similar. The statisticians generally restrict themselves to making inferences about numbers, and consequently their arguments are narrower, more technical and perhaps more rigorous than the philosophers' arguments. But the basic problem is the same. Any valid solution to the problem of statistical inference could at once be applied to the wider philosophical field.

Appendix

At present, Sir Karl Popper (1968) is the philosopher whose theories command the widest attention. The best statistical review is by Hacking (1965), but that book, although very well written, is unavoidably technical. So far as we know, the only attempt to review the statistical problems in a biological context appears as Chapter 7 of Gilbert (1973). Many statisticians would say that both these reviews are slanted towards the views of R. A. Fisher. In particular, Hacking develops an apparently watertight logical basis for Fisher's 'fiducial argument'. That argument transforms probability statements, derived from the data in samples of individuals drawn from some parent population, into probability statements about the statistical parameters of that parent population. It jumps from the *sample* to the *population*. Until Hacking's book appeared, most statisticians thought that in propounding the 'fiducial argument', Fisher had met his Waterloo. Now they are not so sure. The fiducial argument, if valid, overcomes the most knotty of the technical problems of statistical inference; but it applies only to a restricted class of problems, viz. those that admit 'sufficient estimators'.

The usual, and widely accepted, solution to the general problem of scientific inference runs along the following lines. To any proposition, or hypothesis, is assigned a probability. That probability changes in the light of any fresh evidence relevant to the hypothesis. Evidence which tends to discredit a hypothesis reduces its probability; and conversely. The arithmetic rule for calculating the new value of the probability is well established and universally accepted. It is possible for evidence to *negate* a hypothesis, i.e. to make its probability zero: but no amount of evidence can entirely *confirm* a hypothesis, i.e. make its probability equal to one. Therefore, no positive knowledge can ever be entirely certain. Scientific research is then a process of negating some hypotheses and of increasing the probability of others. It is the scientist's responsibility to think up the hypotheses that are to be tested. At the same time, the successful hypotheses may become modified or extended.

Even if this argument is correct, it does not solve the problem of inference, because the meaning of 'probability' has not been defined. Unfortunately, no adequate definition of 'probability' has yet been found. Definitions of probability fall into two main categories. Subjective probabilities are 'degrees of rational belief', i.e. they express the confidence of human beings in the truth of some proposition. By contrast, frequency probabilities measure the frequency of some event. Thus the statement 'the probability that it will rain next Sunday is 75%' is either a statement of belief about a particular Sunday, or a statement of frequency about a class of days, of which next Sunday is a member. Probability may also be defined as a purely mathematical measure, with no obvious application to the real world. Each definition presents its own difficulties, which have so far proved insuperable. Indeed, if a rigorous definition of 'probability', could be found, the problem of inference would *ipso facto* be solved.

Another attempt to solve the problem of inference runs as follows. Inference has worked well in the past: therefore, we may assume that it will still do so in the future. But this argument is itself an inference, and therefore is (at first sight) circular, since it uses an inference to justify the making of inferences. It is possible to cut through the circularity in the following way. It is true that, logically, we can never be perfectly certain of the truth of any proposition whatever; yet human beings do in fact take many things for granted. When the accumulated evidence in favour of some hypothesis becomes overwhelming, the human mind jumps to certainty. This is not a logical thing to do, but it certainly is rational. This 'jump to certainty' may be applied to the argument in the second sentence of this paragraph. Inference has worked so often in the past, that we feel certain that it will work again in the future. We certainly should not trouble to make inferences of some particular kind if they had proved unreliable in the past! If this is indeed the basis on which we rely when making inferences, it implies that inference is strictly non-logical (but rational): in which case, it is hardly surprising that no logical basis has been found. And the argument in this paragraph is not so much a justification for making inferences, as a description of what we actually do.

What has all this got to do with ecological research? Some people contend, quite seriously, that all scientific research must be a mechanical process of erecting and demolishing successive hypotheses. It is true that almost any rational argument can, with sufficient ingenuity, be dressed up as a dialectic. But since the problem of inference is unsolved, no particular recipe for scientific research can be mandatory. The illustrious examples of Madame Curie and Sir Alexander Fleming show that some important discoveries are made by accident. Scientific research is not done by rote. More reasonably, some ecologists argue that ecology has been unsuccessful in the past because of a lack of rigorous hypotheses and theories to be tested. The current outbreak of ecological theorizing, they say, is just what we need to ensure that field work is well directed. It is quite true that ecological research in the past has often involved

Appendix

the mere compilation of species lists, or the aimless collection of data in the hope that something would turn up. On the other hand, theory divorced from reality can only lead to mediaeval scholasticism in its worst sense; and some current ecological theories are dangerously close to that fate. Our strictures in Chapter 1 are directed, not against theory *per se*, but towards theoreticians and laboratory ecologists who announce that they intend to test their hypotheses in the field, but never do so - or who expect others to do so for them. Our own experience shows that ecological relationships in the field work in ways unsuspected by the theoreticians. It therefore seems more profitable to observe how ecological relationships really work, before we begin to theorize about them. But we can have no quarrel with colleagues who prefer to start with abstract hypotheses, *provided that they actually test them in the field*. We have tried to show that such testing is perfectly possible. More than that, we have argued that theorists and analysts must keep their boots dirty, i.e. must themselves participate in field work, if their theories or analyses are to be realistic and sensible. The two extremes of aimless data collection and of theory divorced from reality can only prove sterile: but in between, there are many possible approaches to ecological research. We believe that the approach adopted in this book is productive, and perhaps more productive than most.

REFERENCES

ARNOLD, C. Y. (1960). Maximum-minimum temperatures as a basis for computing heat units. *Proc. Am. Soc. hort. Sci.* 76, 682-92.

BAKER, D. N., HESKETH, J. D. and DUNCAN, W. G. (1972). Simulation of growth and yield in cotton. I. Gross photosynthesis, respiration and growth. *Crop. Sci.* 12, 431-5.

BANKS, J. (1962). *The Endeavour journal of Joseph Banks 1768-1771*, (ed. J. C. Beaglehole). Angus and Robertson, Sydney.

BARTLETT, M. S. and HIORNS, R. W. (eds.) (1973). *Mathematical theory of the dynamics of biological populations*. Academic Press, New York.

BEWICK, T. (1797). *History of British Birds*, vol. 1. Beilby and Bewick, Newcastle.

BIRDSELL, J. B. (1972). *Human evolution*. Rand McNally, Chicago.

BROADHEAD, E. and CHEKE, R. A. (1975). Host spatial pattern, parasitoid interference and the modelling of the dynamics of *Alaptus fusculus* (Hym.: Myrmaridae), a parasitoid of two *Mesopsocus* species (Psocoptera). *J. Anim. Ecol.* 44, 767-93.

CAMPBELL, A., FRAZER, B. D., GILBERT, N., GUTIERREZ, A. P. and MACKAUER, M. (1974). Temperature requirements of some aphids and their parasites. *J. appl. Ecol.* 11, 431-8.

CARL, E. A. (1970). The regulation of numbers in *Tribolium confusum* by means of selective migration. Ph.D. thesis, University of British Columbia, Vancouver.

CAUGHLEY, G. (1966). Mortality patterns in mammals. *Ecology* 47, 906-18.

CHARNOV, E. L. and KREBS, J. R. (1974). On clutch-size and fitness. *Ibis* 116, 217-19.

COALE, A. J. (1972). *Growth and structure of human populations*. Princeton University Press, Princeton.

CROFT, B. A. and THOMPSON, W. W. (1976). Integrated control of apple mites. *Ext. Bull. Mich. St. Univ. Ext. Publ.* (in press).

DEBACH, P. (1974). *Biological control by natural enemies*. Cambridge University Press, Cambridge.

DEMPSTER, J. P. (1971). The population ecology of the cinnabar moth, *Tyria jacobaeae* L. (Lepidoptera, Arctiidae). *Oecologia* 7, 26-67.

DOUTT, R. L. (1964). The historical development of biological control. In *The biological control of insect pests and weeds*, pp. 21-42. Reinhold, New York.

EBERHARD, M. J. W. (1975). The evolution of social behaviour by kin selection. *Q. Rev. Biol.* 50, 1-33.

EHRLICH, P. R., WHITE, R. R., SINGER, M. C., MCKECHNIE, S. W. and

References

GILBERT, L. E. (1975). Checkerspot butterflies: a historical perspective. *Science, N.Y.* **188**, 221-8.

EL-SHARKAWY, M., HESKETH, J. D. and MURAMOTO, H. (1965). Leaf photosynthetic rates and other growth characteristics among 26 species of *Gossypium. Crop Sci.* **5**, 173-5.

ELTON, C. S. (1966). *The pattern of animal communities.* Methuen, London.

EVANS, L. T. (ed.) (1975). *Crop physiology.* Cambridge University Press, Cambridge.

FALCON, L. A., VAN DEN BOSCH, R., GALLAGHER, J. and DAVIDSON, A. (1971). Investigation of the pest status of *Lygus hesperus* in cotton in central California. *J. econ. Ent.* **64**, 56-61.

FISHER, R. A. (1930). *The genetical theory of natural selection.* Clarendon Press, Oxford.

FRAZER, B. D. and FORBES, A. R. (1968). *Masonaphis maxima* (Mason) (Homoptera: Aphididae), an aphid on thimbleberry with an unusual life history. *J. ent. Soc. Brit. Columbia* **65**, 36-9.

FRAZER, B. D. and GILBERT, N. (1976). Coccinellids and aphids. *J. entomol. Soc. Brit. Col.* **73** (in press).

FRAZER, B. D. and VAN DEN BOSCH, R. (1973). Biological control of the walnut aphid in California: the interrelationship of the aphid and its parasite. *Envir. ent.* **2**, 561-8.

GIESE, R. L., PEART, R. M. and HUBER, R. T. (1975). Pest management. *Science, N.Y.* **187**, 1045-52.

GILBERT, L. E. (1975). Ecological consequences of a coevolved mutualism between butterflies and plants. *Coevolution of animals and plants* (eds. L. E. Gilbert and P. H. Raven) University of Texas Press, Austin.

GILBERT, L. E. and SINGER, M. C. (1973). Dispersal and gene flow in a butterfly species. *Am. Nat.* **107**, 58-72.

GILBERT, N. (1973). *Biometrical interpretation.* Clarendon Press, Oxford.

GILBERT, N. and GUTIERREZ, A. P. (1973). A plant-aphid-parasite relationship. *J. Anim. Ecol.* **42**, 323-40.

GILBERT, N. and HUGHES, R. D. (1971). A model of an aphid population - three adventures. *J. Anim. Ecol.* **40**, 525-34.

GUTIERREZ, A. P., CHRISTENSEN, J., MERRITT, C. M., LOEW, W., SUMMERS, C. G. and COTHRAN, W. R. (1976). Alfalfa and the Egyptian alfalfa weevil. *Can. Ent.* (in press).

GUTIERREZ, A. P., DENTON, W. H., SHADE, R., MALTBY, H., BURGER, T. and MOOREHEAD, G. (1974). The within-field dynamics of the cereal leaf beetle (*Oulema melanopus* (L.)) in wheat and oats. *J. Anim. Ecol.* **43**, 627-40.

GUTIERREZ, A. P., FALCON, L. A., LOEW, W., LEIPZIG, P. A. and VAN DEN BOSCH, R. (1975). An analysis of cotton production in California: a model for Acala cotton and the effects of defoliators on its yields. *Envir. Ent.* **4**, 125-36.

GUTIERREZ, A. P., HAVENSTEIN, D. E., NIX, H. and MOORE, P. A. (1974).

The ecology of *Aphis craccivora* Koch and subterranean clover stunt virus in south-east Australia. II. A model of cowpea aphid populations in temperate pastures. *J. appl. Ecol.* **11**, 1-20.

✓ HACKING, I. (1965). *Logic of statistical inference.* Cambridge University Press, Cambridge.

✓ HAGEN, K. S. (1974). The significance of predacious *Coccinellidae* in biological and integrated control of insects. *Entomophaga Mem. H. S.* **7**, 25-44.

HAGEN, K. S. and VAN DEN BOSCH, R. (1968). Impact of pathogens, parasites and predators on aphids. *A. Rev. Ent.* **13**, 325-84.

HARPER, J. L. and WHITE, J. (1971). The dynamics of plant populations. In Dynamics of populations. (eds. P. J. den Boer and G. R. Gradwell). *Proc. Adv. Study Inst. Dynamics Numbers Popul. (Oosterbeek)*, 41-63.

HASSELL, M. P. (1969). A population model for the interaction between *Cyzenis albicans* (Fall.) (Tachinidae) and *Operophtera brumata* (L.) (Geometridae) at Wytham, Berkshire. *J. Anim. Ecol.* **38**, 567-76.

HASSELL, M. P. and MAY, R. M. (1973). Stability in insect host-parasite models. *J. Anim. Ecol.* **42**, 693-726.

HESKETH, J. D., BAKER, D. N. and DUNCAN, W. G. (1971). Simulation of growth and yield of cotton. Respiration and the carbon balance. *Crop Sci.* **11**, 394-8.

HOLLING, C. S. (1965). The functional response of predators to prey density and its role in mimicry and population regulation. *Mem. ent. Soc. Can.* **45**, 1-60.

HOLLING, C. S. (1966). The functional response of invertebrate predators to prey density. *Mem. ent. Soc. Can* **48**, 1-86.

HOLLING, C. S. (1973). Resilience and stability of ecological systems. *Ann. rev. Ecol. and Systematics* **4**, 1-23.

HUGHES, R. D. (1955). The influence of the prevailing weather on the numbers of *Meromyza variegata* Meigen (Diptera, Chloropidae) caught with a sweepnet. *J. Anim. Ecol.* **24**, 324-35.

✓ HUGHES, R. D. (1963). Population dynamics of the cabbage aphid, *Brevicoryne brassicae* (L.) *J. Anim. Ecol.* **32**, 393-424.

HUGHES, R. D. and GILBERT, N. (1968). A model of an aphid population - a general statement. *J. Anim. Ecol.* **37**, 553-63.

HUGHES, R. D. and NICHOLAS, W. L. (1974). The spring migration of the bushfly (*Musca vetustissima* Walk.): evidence of displacement provided by natural population markers including parasitism. *J. Anim. Ecol.* **43**, 411-28.

JONES, R. E. (1976*a*). Search behaviour: a study of three caterpillar species. *Behaviour* **61** (in press).

JONES, R. E. (1976*b*). Movement patterns and egg distributions of cabbage butterflies. (To be published.)

JONES, R. E. (1976*c*). Movement patterns and the population dynamics of cabbage butterflies. (To be published.)

KENNEDY, J. S. and STROYAN, H. L. G. (1959). Biology of aphids. *A. Rev.*

References

Ent. **4**, 139-60.

KREBS, C. J., KELLER, B. L. and TAMARIN, R. H. (1969). *Microtus* population biology: demographic changes in fluctuating populations of *M. ochrogaster* and *M. pennsylvanicus* in southern Indiana. *Ecology* **50**, 587-607.

LACK, D. L. (1954). *The natural regulation of animal numbers.* Clarendon Press, Oxford.

LACK, D. L. (1966). *Population studies of birds.* Clarendon Press, Oxford.

MACKAUER, M. and VAN DEN BOSCH, R. (1973). Quantitative evaluation of natural enemy effectiveness: general applicability of evaluation results. *J. appl. Ecol.* **10**, 330-35.

MAELZER, D. (1976). The biology and main causes of change in numbers in the rose-aphid *Macrosiphum rosae* (L.) in South Australia. (To be published.)

MANLY, B. F. J. (1974). A comparison of methods for the analysis of insect stage-frequency data. *Oecologia* **17**, 335-48.

MCARTHUR, J. A., HESKETH, J. D. and BAKER, D. N. (1975). *Cotton.* In Evans (1975) *(op. cit.).*

MCKINION, J. M., JONES, J. W. and HESKETH, J. D. (1974). Analysis of SIMCOT: photosynthesis and growth. *Beltwide Cotton Prod. Res. Conf. Es. Proc., Memphis*, 118-25.

MILLER, D. R. (1974). Sensitivity analysis and validation of simulation models. *J. theor. Biol.* **48**, 345-60.

MORAN, P. A. P. (1962). *The statistical processes of evolutionary theory.* Clarendon Press, Oxford.

MORRIS, R. F. (1955). The development of sampling techniques for forest insect defoliators, with particular reference to the spruce budworm. *Can. J. Zool.* **33**, 225-94.

MORRIS, R. F. (ed.) (1963). The dynamics of epidemic spruce budworm populations. *Mem. ent. Soc. Can.* **31**, 1-332.

MORRIS, R. F. (1971). Observed and simulated changes in genetic quality in natural populations of *Hyphantria cunea. Can. Ent.* **103**, 893-906.

MORRIS, R. F. and BENNETT, C. W. (1967). Seasonal population trends and extensive census methods for *Hyphantria cunea. Can. Ent.* **99**, 9-17.

MYERS, K. (1971). The rabbit in Australia. In Dynamics of populations. (eds. P. J. den Boer and G. R. Gradwell.) *Proc. Adv. Study Inst. Dynamics Numbers Popul. (Oosterbeek)*, 478-506.

MYERS, K. and PARKER, B. S. (1975). A study of the biology of the wild rabbit in climatically different regions of eastern Australia. VI. Changes in numbers and distribution related to climate and land systems in semiarid north-western New South Wales. *Aust. Wildl. Research* **2**, 11-32.

NEUENSCHWANDER, P. (1975). Influence of temperature and humidity on the immature stages of *Hemerobius pacificus. Envir. Ent.* **4**, 215-20.

NEUENSCHWANDER, P., HAGEN, K. S. and SMITH, R. F. (1975). Predation of aphids in California's alfalfa fields. *Hilgardia* **43**, 53-78.

NICHOLSON, A. J. (1933). The balance of animal populations. *J. Anim.*

Ecol. **2**, 131-78.

PARKER, F. D. and PINNELL, R. E. (1972). Further studies of the biological control of *Pieris rapae* using supplemental host and parasite releases. *Envir. Ent.* **1**, 150-7.

POPPER, K. R. (1968). *The logic of scientific discovery.* 3rd edn. Hutchinson, London.

RABINOVICH, J. E. (1972). Simulación en una computadora digital de la regulacion poblacional de triatominos vectores de la enfermedad de Chagas por parte del parasíto *Telenomus fariai* (Hymenoptera: Scelionidae), y de las estrategias para el control integrado. *Anales el 1er Congresso Latinoamericano de Entomologia. Cuzco,* Peru, 12-18 Abril, 1971.

REGEV, U., GUTIERREZ, A. P. and FEDER, G. (1976). Pests as a common property resource: a case study in the control of the Egyptian alfalfa weevil. *Amer. J. agric. Econ.* (in press).

RICE, R. W., MORRIS, J. G., MAEDA, B. T. and BALDWIN, R. L. (1974). Simulation of animal functions in models of production systems: ruminants on the range. *Fed. Proc.* **33**, 188-95.

ROYAMA, T. (1971). A comparative study of models for predation and parasitism. *Res. popul. Ecol. Kyoto Univ. Suppl.* **1**.

RUESINK, W. G. (1976). Status of the systems approach to pest management. *A. Rev. Ent.* **21**, 27-44.

SAAKYAN-BARANOVA, A. A., SUGONJAEV, E. S. and SHELDESHOVA, G. G. (1971). *Akatsievaya lozhnoshchitovka i ee parazity.* Izdatelstvo Nauka, Leningrad.

SINCLAIR, A. R. E. (1974). The natural regulation of buffalo populations in East Africa. III. Population trends and mortality. *E. Afr. Wild. J.* **12**, 185-200.

SINIFF, D. B. and JESSEN, C. R. (1969). A simulation model of animal movement patterns. *Adv. ecol. Res.* **6**, 185-219.

SOUTHWOOD, T. R. E. (1966). *Ecological methods.* Methuen, London.

STINNER, R. E., GUTIERREZ, A. P. and BUTLER, G. D. (1974). An algorithm for temperature-dependent growth rate simulation. *Can. Ent.* **106**, 519-24.

STINNER, R. E., RABB, R. L. and BRADLEY, J. R. (1974). Population dynamics of *Heliothis zea* (Boddie) and *H. virescens* (F.) in North Carolina: a simulation model. *Envir. Ent.* **3**, 163-8.

STREIFER, W. (1974). Realistic models in population ecology. *Adv. ecol. Res.* **8**, 199-266.

TAYLOR, L. R. (1975). Longevity, fecundity and size: control of reproductive potential in a polymorphic migrant, *Aphis fabae* Scop. *J. Anim. Ecol.* **44**, 135-63.

TAYLOR, L. R., FRENCH, R. A. and MACAULAY, E. D. M. (1973). Low-altitude migration and diurnal flight periodicity: the importance of *Plusia gamma* L. (Lepidoptera: Plusiidae). *J. Anim. Ecol.* **42**, 751-60.

THOMPSON, W. R. (1924). La théorie mathématique de l'action des

References

parasites entomophages et le facteur du hasard. *Annls. Fac. Sci. Marseille* **2**, 69–89.

USHER, M. B. and WILLIAMSON, M. H. (eds) (1974). *Ecological stability.* Chapman and Hall, London.

VAN DEN BOSCH, R. and MESSENGER, P. S. (1973). *Biological control.* Intext Educational Publishers, New York.

VARLEY, G. C., GRADWELL, G. R. and HASSELL, M. P. (1973). *Insect population ecology.* Blackwell, Oxford.

WATSON, A. and JENKINS, D. (1968). Experiments on population control by territorial behaviour in red grouse. *J. Anim. Ecol.* **37**, 595–614.

WATT, K. E. F. (1968). *Ecology and resource management.* McGraw-Hill, New York.

WAY, M. J. (1973). Objectives, methods and scope of integrated control. In Insects: studies in population management. (eds P. W. Geier, L. R. Clark, D. J. Anderson and H. A. Nix.) *Ecol. Soc. Aust. Mem.* **1**, 138–52.

WAY, M. J. and CAMMELL, M. E. (1971). Self-regulation in animal populations. In Dynamics of populations. (eds P. J. den Boer and G. R. Gradwell). *Proc. Adv. Study Inst. Dynamics Numbers Popul. (Oosterbeek)*, 232–42.

WELLINGTON, W. G. (1964). Qualitative changes in populations in unstable environments. *Can. Ent.* **96**, 436–51.

WILLIAMS, G. C. (ed.) (1971). *Group selection.* Aldine Atherton, Chicago.

WILSON, A. G. L., HUGHES, R. D. and GILBERT, N. (1972). The response of cotton to pest attack. *Bull. ent. Res.* **61**, 405–14.

WOOD, B. J. (1971). Development of integrated control programs for pests of tropical perennial crops in Malaysia. In *Biological control* (ed. C. B. Huffaker), pp. 422–57. Plenum, New York.

WRATTEN, S. D. (1973). The effectiveness of the coccinellid beetle, *Adalia bipunctata* (L.), as a predator of the lime aphid, *Eucallipterus tiliae* L. *J. Anim. Ecol.* **42**, 785–802.

INDEX OF NAMES

Index of Names

INDEX OF SUBJECTS